# THE AGES
# OF GIELGUD

David Hockney
*Sir John Gielgud* 1974
Ink drawing
42.5 × 33 cm/16¾ × 13 in.

# THE AGES
# OF GIELGUD

## AN ACTOR AT EIGHTY

EDITED BY

## RONALD HARWOOD

HODDER AND STOUGHTON
LONDON SYDNEY AUCKLAND TORONTO

The still from *The Secret Agent* appears by courtesy of the Rank Organisation PLC, that from *Julius Caesar* by courtesy of Metro-Goldwyn-Mayer, and that from *The Charge of the Light Brigade* by courtesy of Woodfall America.

Sir John Gielgud kindly allowed the editor to select pictures for this book from his own albums. It has not always been possible to trace copyright. The publishers apologise for any inadvertent infringement and will be happy to include an acknowledgment in any future edition.

The Chronology has been expanded from Ronald Hayman's 1971 version published in his biography, *John Gielgud*. The publishers wish to thank Mr Hayman and also Richard Findlater for their help in updating the list.

Sir Alec Guinness's contribution is a version of an article that will appear in a collection of autobiographical pieces to be published by Hamish Hamilton.

*British Library Cataloguing in Publication Data*

The Ages of Gielgud.
  1. Gielgud, John    2. Actors – Great Britain
  – Biography
  I. Harwood, Ronald
  792'028'0924     PN2598.G45

ISBN 0-340-34828-3

# CONTENTS

# ILLUSTRATIONS

*Richard II*, Old Vic, 1929
Lino-cut by Pauline Logan

# INTRODUCTION

# INTRODUCTION
## RONALD HARWOOD

Arthur John Gielgud was born on April 14th, 1904, in London. His mother, Kate, was related to the Terrys, one of the most illustrious English theatrical clans; his father, Frank Gielgud, English-born, was of Polish parentage. Their third son was educated at Westminster and, for the theatre, at the Benson Dramatic School and the Royal Academy of Dramatic Art. He made his first appearance on the stage at the Old Vic in November 1921. Almost exactly five years later, aged twenty-two, he replaced Noël Coward as Lewis Dodd in *The Constant Nymph* in the West End. For almost sixty years he has been a leading theatrical figure and a dominant force in the English–speaking theatre of this century.

I have deliberately set down the bare facts in a staccato monotone (reminiscent of those brief biographies at the back of theatre programmes) to make two points. The first is that Gielgud's family background, early success, speedy fulfilment of promise and astonishing staying-power emphasise what may be thought of as an effortless flight of glory. He never had to endure, for example, the hard slog of an actor such as Henry Irving who in his first three years on the stage played four hundred and twenty-eight characters, mostly in the provinces, and had to wait fifteen years before London acknowledged his gifts. The second and, for me, the more important point is to draw attention to Gielgud's remarkable adaptability, one aspect of which can be simply illustrated: besides his enrichment of the classical reper-toire, Gielgud's long professional life has enabled him to interpret, either as actor or director, many of the most renowned playwrights of the day, men with whom he was or is contemporary. The incomplete list in itself dramatises the span: Bernard Shaw, Noël Coward, Emlyn Williams, André Obey, W. Somerset Maugham, Tennessee Williams, Christopher Fry, N. C. Hunter, Graham Greene, Peter Shaffer, Terence Rattigan, Edward Albee, David Storey, Charles Wood, Harold Pinter.

That span embraces the decades which social historians tell us have produced the most rapid changes in human history. Gielgud first saw the light of day in the reign of King Edward VII, at 7 Gledhow Gardens, just off the Old Brompton Road in South Kensington. Frank and Kate Gielgud employed a German governess and a staff of servants to help with the upbringing of their four children, Lewis, Val, Arthur John and Eleanor. It was a superior home in a superior part of London, respectable, secure and, I suspect, uncomfortable as only the English upper-middle class understand the meaning of the word. Gielgud himself has described the house as steep and chilly, recalling with particular distaste the icy rooms, the tepid baths, the chill linoleum which covered the floors; he looked forward to being ill when he would be allowed a hip bath and the luxury of a big towel being warmed on the fender of the nursery fire.

But young Arthur John was to know luxury of another and more important kind: the comfort of a secure world. It was an age when a family such as the Gielguds could be certain of their place in the social pattern. It would be known exactly what was expected of them and what they, in turn, expected. In his autobiography, *Early Stages*, he writes graphically of his privileged childhood, yet he also reveals a certain nervousness and self-obsession which can with hindsight be interpreted as acute symptoms of an actor's temperament. For Gielgud's inheritance, and the one upon which his future was to depend, was more enduring and pervasive than even the English class system. He was born into the English Theatre.

It was as if Gielgud's talent was deliberately bred and not the result of an accident of birth. Few actors in the almost unbroken English tradition which has lasted over five hundred years can have had such a splendid pedigree. His maternal ancestry is the line to which he himself draws greatest attention, perhaps with some justification. For more than a hundred years the Terry family have been members of the English theatrical aristocracy, although their beginnings were humble enough. They make their first entrance in the late 1830s, the decade in which Victoria ascended to the throne. Benjamin, the son of a Portsmouth publican, wed Sarah Ballard and went on the stage. Their marriage lasted fifty-four years until Sarah's death in 1892. In that time they produced eleven children, seven of whom followed their parents' calling. By the close of the century, the family name was made famous by the success of their daughters, Kate and Ellen, and their youngest son, Fred (1864–1932), a popular actor-manager, the epitome of Terry charm, famed for his performances in *The Scarlet Pimpernel* and *Henry of Navarre*.

But it was Kate who was the first of the Terrys to achieve prominence when, in 1858, aged fourteen, her portrayal of Cordelia brought her instant stardom. For the next nine years she played in London and the provinces; once, in Manchester, she acted with the then unknown Henry Irving. At the age of twenty-three, she retired from the stage to marry Arthur Lewis. Her farewell as Juliet at the Adelphi, London, played to packed houses. In time, four daughters were born. The eldest was also called Kate.

Irving was to play a more important role in the life of Kate Terry's sister, Ellen, one of the legendary figures in English theatrical history. A woman of astonishing beauty – the kind of beauty which transcends fashion and faded photographs – she was also an actress of the highest order. In 1878, aged thirty-one, she accepted Irving's invitation to be his leading lady. Their partnership lasted twenty-four years, and it is now thought to have been more than just a professional relationship. No proof, however, has ever come to light; seeing each other every evening of their lives no doubt relieved them of the need to write indiscreet *billets-doux* for posterity to savour.

Discretion and the longing for respectability were, perhaps, more deeply rooted in Irving than in his leading lady. Before she joined him at the Lyceum, Ellen had, aged sixteen, entered into what was to prove a disastrous marriage to the artist, G. F. Watts. Later, she caused a scandal by running away to live with Edward Godwin and having children by him. All the more remarkable must have been her talent for the public to adore her as it did. With Irving she helped to create the standards and style of theatrical presentation that were to stand as the foundation stone of the English stage until the second half of the twentieth century.

(Her illegitimate son, Gordon Craig, was to rebel against the Theatre of Good Taste which his mother and Irving represented, and was one of the secret forces that caused that edifice to crack.)

In 1895, Irving was knighted, the first actor to receive the accolade. Ellen had to wait a good deal longer for official recognition. It may have been that her youthful indiscretions had not been forgotten or forgiven. In 1925, three years before her death, she was made a Dame Grand Cross of the British Empire.

Into this brilliant theatrical world Arthur John Gielgud was born and it was the Edwardian theatre he inherited, reverenced, and which in time he was to transform. Miss Kate Lewis – Ellen's niece and not an actress – provided the Terry link. In 1893, aged twenty-seven, she married a young stockbroker with a peculiar name, Frank Gielgud, born in England, the son of Polish parents who could themselves boast a distinguished theatrical lineage.

It is less well known, and less remarked on, that John Gielgud's great-grandmother on his father's side was an important European actress. She was of sufficient renown to be celebrated by a marble bust in the foyer of the Opera House at Lvov. Of his Polish ancestry, Gielgud recalls:

> My grandparents on my father's side were both Polish but spoke perfect English, and my great-grandmother, Aniela Aszpergerowa, had been a successful actress in Lithuania, famous for her Shakespearean roles. Her husband Wojciech was also a famous leading actor. Their daughter married Adam Gielgud, my grandfather . . .

He goes on, however, to doubt the importance of the Polish connection. But Marguerite Steen, the author of the Terry family history, *A Pride of Terrys*, takes a different view:

> Physically, he bears no faintest resemblance to any member of his Terry . . . family . . . John Gielgud is markedly lacking in Terry characteristics, particularly on the male side . . .
>
> John Gielgud inherits almost equal parts of English and Polish blood, the latter coming out strongly in his appearance, and to a notable degree colouring his acting. For obvious reasons it was clearly detectable in the Russian play and in

*Richard of Bordeaux;*\* it appeared in *Noah*.† I venture to think that none of those parts could have been played in that particular way by an all-British actor. Its beat is audible in his verse speaking.

It is, of course, dangerous to play the game of national characteristics, but I, too, incline towards Marguerite Steen's theory. Geographical boundaries do seem to ensure that certain modes of physique, behaviour, expression and feeling are stamped to greater or lesser degree on succeeding generations. I have seen every leading English actor in a variety of roles since the early 1950s, and Gielgud alone has a powerful soulfulness which seems to me decidedly un-English. In his early days on the stage, he was accused of being over-emotional; he has himself admitted to being able to cry at the turn of the tap. (The Terrys, it is true, were not unknown for this useful facility.) But I believe the fusion of Anglo-Saxon and Slav to be one of the clues to understanding Gielgud's fascinating qualities both as an actor and as a man: his insights into comedy and tragedy, his elegant wit and emotional depths, his gregariousness and aloofness, the rapid shifts of mood, the radiant smile and the sadness in his eyes.

To meet Gielgud now, or to watch him act, is to doubt the authenticity of his birth certificate. I first saw him in London in 1952, as Leontes in *The Winter's Tale* (a portrayal I still regard as one of the four or five great performances I have witnessed). He was forty-eight then, slender, passionate, electrifying. I stood at the stage door of the Phoenix Theatre off Charing Cross Road and watched him emerge, springing not walking to a car, talking at terrific speed to a friend, dazzling those of us who waited with a smile that seemed to shine even while he continued to chatter. Jump the years: 1965, again the Phoenix, this time as Chekhov's Ivanov. There he is, over sixty now, slender, passionate, electrifying. Ten years later, I detected a change for the first time, or so I thought. In *No Man's Land* by Harold Pinter, in 1975, as Spooner, I believed that Gielgud was beginning to play his age. But it was about then that I met him for the first time, and realised

---

\* by Gordon Daviot, 1933. One of Gielgud's great early successes. Gordon Daviot (1897–1952) was the pseudonym of Elizabeth Mackintosh who also wrote novels under the name of Josephine Tey (*The Daughter of Time*).

† by André Obey (1892–1975). Directed in 1935 by Michel Saint-Denis (1897–1971), influential French teacher and director who worked in England.

very quickly that Spooner was, in fact, to Gielgud a character part. In person, I discovered, he was slender, passionate, electrifying. He walked and talked at terrific speed. He had seen most of the plays and films in London, read the latest books, visited the art exhibitions and was cast down by the thought that he might soon be out of work. And when he banished that unreasonable but probably habitual concern from his mind, his smile dazzled.

Spooner was, incidentally, the first time I had seen him *impersonate* a character, immersing himself in the externals of a part as well as following the interior map. In the past, Gielgud's preoccupation as an actor, it seemed, was almost totally with the inner life of a character, but in the Pinter play he was showing the world in no uncertain manner that an old dog can learn a great many new tricks. It was yet another mark of his adaptability.

Perhaps I do Gielgud an unintentional disservice by repeating that word adaptability, for it could be argued that an actor, to be the mirror of his time, must simply follow fashion to stay in the limelight. After all, nothing could be easier than to pay lip-service to whatever audiences and critics find most attractive at any given moment, and then hope for the best. But one of the measures of a true artist is not simply the desire to move and dally with the times, but rather the need to remain true to personal standards in a changing world. That has been Gielgud's way: he has stood centre stage, a beacon of integrity, while the scenery was shifted behind him.

This book is by way of a tribute to that abiding quality on the occasion of John Gielgud's eightieth birthday. The pieces are written by friends, colleagues and critics; they cover much of his life and career from young leading man to what *Time* magazine described as Major Movie Star; they are personal accounts of the actor, the man of the theatre, the artist and the man.

# JC
# TREWIN

## J C TREWIN

In 1928, John Gielgud appeared in a farce, *Holding Out The Apple* with Hermione Baddeley. It was the first time he saw his name in lights, and the first time a young provincial journalist, J. C. Trewin, saw Gielgud on the stage. Trewin (b. 1908) went on to make a distinguished name for himself as a drama critic, chiefly of the *Birmingham Post* and the *Illustrated London News* (since 1946). He was literary editor of the *Observer* and the paper's second dramatic critic, 1943–53. He is also the author of a great many books on the theatre.

# JC TREWIN

It is always a tribute to an actor when younger actors, knowingly or unknowingly, seek to imitate his voice. Thus, during the 1930s, you heard minor Gielguds everywhere, though they had little more success than a trickling waterfall has when it tries to be a cascade: Lodore during drought. If you listen, you can still find that optimistic waterfall from time to time. John Gielgud's own voice, the unexampled original, belongs to the ages: it has interpreted the theatre for me through well over half a century.

I heard it first – autobiography creeping in – near midsummer in what seems to have been the hot June of 1928, one of those things probably fatal to check. Let it stay as a hot June. A nineteen-year-old, desperately stage-struck, on leave from a newspaper in the South-West, I crammed as many plays as possible into six days, afternoons and evenings. Most mornings were spent round the West End theatres, forty or so, examining their photographs with an infra-red eagerness, wondering why some were smaller and less well placed than the others; studying playbills and asking, just as naively, why our local Rep could not have had this unblotched printing; and once or twice entering a foyer to look at its décor – never very tingling – and the size of the queue, if any, at the guichet. The most rewarding was the big foyer of His Majesty's, dominated, I believe, by a portrait of Beerbohm Tree's* King John; but I ranged freely to such outliers

* Sir Herbert Beerbohm Tree (1853–1917), actor-manager who built Her Majesty's Theatre in the Haymarket, London in 1896–7.

as the Kingsway, the Playhouse, and the Royalty in Dean Street. Even, and unprofitably, to the Scala.

A first night was announced (over four decades before the preview habit would complicate theatre chronology). No matinée that day. I attached myself to an unexpectedly thin line for the Globe pit off Shaftesbury Avenue: a piece called *Holding Out the Apple* by a dramatist unfamiliar to me then or since, but one of the light comedies – this was, dangerously, "a comedy with a catch in it" – that abounded in the Avenue. I remember casual things: for the queue's benefit, a glum paper-tearer who produced from alleged sheets of the day's *Times* a more or less precise image of Buckingham Palace; within the Globe itself a low wooden barrier to separate stalls from pit; a free programme, which struck me as almost insensate generosity; and the small-talk of my neighbour, a young engineer from Newcastle-upon-Tyne, who was a splendid audience and indeed led most of the night's laughter.

Not that there was much laughter to lead. From this distance I bring back vaguely a middle-aged character-actor, Paul Gill, and, far from vaguely, a tall, slim young man, facially like a gentle eaglet, with the swift silver flash of a tenor voice that has sounded through the decades. He had, I knew, succeeded Noël Coward two years previously as Lewis Dodd in *The Constant Nymph*: I was uncertain how to pronounce his name. Now he had nothing memorable to do or say: I cannot even recall the line that has given him so much recollected agony: "You have a way of holding out the apple that positively gives me the pip." Applause was mild, apart from my neighbour's staunch approval; for some reason he wrung my hand at the end. Within an hour or two, little of the night (certainly not the catch in it) lingered, only a voice that appeared to have shone in the wrong play; the still oddly unrelaxed bearing of its owner; and the name Gielgud in my diary. The actor was twenty-four.

No prophet, I could not have said that John Gielgud would come one day to symbolise for us the English stage of well over half a century. But we would listen to him growing into history through the 1930s when, more than anybody, he gave shape and coherence to a West End medley; through intermittent splendours behind the war-time black-out; and on again through all those expressions of the Actors', Dramatists', and Directors' Theatres as label followed label and fashion destroyed fashion.

Always there was Gielgud's voice. I heard it a second time during the ebb of a winter holiday, a night in 1929 when – still a regional explorer – I discovered the Old Vic, just set, under Harcourt Williams,* upon one of its most famous periods. I got there with a minute to spare, diving into a coffee-scented underworld and climbing to an auditorium that kept what Alan Pryce-Jones had not yet called its fringe of plaster lace. The legendary Lilian Baylis,† so another talkative neighbour assured me, was leaning from her box. The play was *A Midsummer Night's Dream*; it would not have been surprising if she had taken a final call. (But Harcourt Williams did.) Presently, wandering up Waterloo Road towards eleven o'clock, I thought of the mound in the centre of the Wood near Athens over which the lovers had to scramble. Most of all, I remembered the silver authority and the patrician tones, the Terry voice, of John Gielgud, unchanged in quality over eighteen months but now in a new dimension. A regal Oberon, he was able to enjoy the mischief of the haunted grove. One day he would be grimmer; but now, most of a lifetime away, I see him standing, mooncast King of Shadows, urgently bending forward as he ordered Leslie French's‡ Puck to look for Helena, "By some illusion see thou bring her here," and listening affectionately to the answer, "I go, I go" – with French's peevish emphasis, "*Look*, how I go!" I caught the night train to Plymouth, startled by a new experience.

It was new for someone used to what a cynical schoolmaster had described as "a sonority of Shakespeare", touring companies, several of them, "pomping folk" in South Cornwall dialect, that as a rule held to a tempo resolutely slow. Now in Waterloo Road I had found a production that danced like quicksilver; at its core an actor who animated language and movement as Garrick must have done when he came into the traditional world of James Quin.ø

The Old Vic efflorescence at the end of the 1920s is seen now as a historic event. Engaged elsewhere, I was disappointed to lose

---

* Harcourt Williams (1880–1957), producer at the Old Vic 1929–34, where he staged nearly fifty productions.

† Lilian Baylis (1874–1937), founder of the Old Vic and Sadler's Wells companies.

‡ Leslie French (b. 1904), actor, the definitive Puck between the wars.

ø After Garrick's debut, Quin, an actor of the old school, said, 'If this young man be right, then we have all been wrong.'

Gielgud's Richard II which Harcourt Williams would praise as "a tall willowy figure in black velvet, surmounted by a fair head, the pale agonised face set beneath a glittering crown." Very far from Garrick who would hear no word of Richard, and who wrote eccentrically, in the fading of his career, to the editor, George Steevens: "It is one of the least interesting of the Historical plays – it will not do."

Curiously (living in London now), Richard was the next part I saw Gielgud play, not in Shakespeare's text but in the serviceable prose of a Scottish dramatist, Gordon Daviot's *Richard of Bordeaux*. Coming back to the West End stage after those Vic seasons when he had been the youngest Hamlet and Lear of his period, Gielgud, it seemed, soon had the London stage growing about him at the New (now the Albery) in St Martin's Lane. Though at its simplest, *Richard of Bordeaux* was a romantic tapestry, Gielgud's elegiac sense, the tones that could glorify a plain prose statement, and the intuitive knowledge – an ancestral gift – of what would, or would not, go in performance, made all the night glitter. He suggested once that the dramatist had "improved on Shakespeare (from a commercial point of view at any rate) by giving Richard a sense of humour". At that hour in the West End, no doubt, though the idea had hardly occurred to me.

Across the 1930s, a mixed, wayward, restless decade, John Gielgud stood on the crest – often as "producer", today's "director", as well as leading man. After *Richard* many people were asking why he did not return to Shakespeare – I recall a wave of letters tumbling into the London daily newspaper where I worked – and in 1934 he replied with his own New Theatre revival of *Hamlet*. I have an impression of autumnal bronze in its sets; against them the marvellous young Hamlet – they were not generally young – whose voice was a Stradivarius controlled by a master. He could have been born into Elsinore as the lonely Prince. Some people, I know, were wistful for the unmatch'd form and stature of blown youth from the Vic in the spring of 1930 (not, after all, a long gap), but this I had merely read about. The New Theatre *Hamlet*, recreated with the actor's mind and nerves, fastidiously scored, would be in its pace, emotion, breeding, and what the eighteenth century used to call "transitions" – here never awkwardly stressed – the major classic performance of its day. It was a man profoundly hurt, profoundly searching: the work, though Gielgud might, and would, deny the term, of a romantic intellectual: the courtier's, soldier's, scholar's, eye, tongue, sword. ("I'm not sure," Graham Robertson ★ wrote in a letter to a friend, "that his loveliest moment is not his happy, laughing death. His terrible job is over, all the worrying people are dead, he himself is dying, and at last he can relax.")

Hamlet – unequalled among the seventy and more I have met – was the newest prize from a family destined, in various moods, to lead the British stage. I am unsure what the Terry name means now. Fifty years ago it meant a great deal. To be a Terry is to be a connoisseur of the theatre; to impose style upon any text, however superficially baffling. Style is not a physical affectation. It is bred of a natural elegance of mind, an unblurred response to the word. John Gielgud, in those burgeoning years, may have had his mannerisms, indulgences in gait and gesture, occasionally in a vocal cadence; but he had long taught himself to speak. ("His quality is almost frightening," the veteran actress, Dorothy Green, said to me a year before her death.) He said himself, "I try to study the sound, shape, and length of words as they are written on the page. In a verse speech (and often in a long prose one, too) I am constantly aware of the whole span of the arc – the beginning, middle, and end of the passage." We were never so aware of this, I think, as in the advice to the Players which could have been, though nobody can tell us, Shakespeare's and Burbage's personal comment on Edward Alleyn and his school of sound-and-fury.

It is the New Theatre *Hamlet* – "This is I, Hamlet the Dane" – that dwells unflawed. I would see the play again in the immediate pre-war summer of 1939 before Gielgud took his company (Fay Compton the latest Ophelia) out to the Kronborg courtyard at Elsinore: it would be the last stage production in the building that, long ago, retaining the portico and some of the back wall, had succeeded Irving's Lyceum. Though doubtless the portrait had changed in detail since 1934, his Hamlet had for me fixed itself firmly in a single night, as great performances – and there are not many of these – have a habit of doing.

★ Graham Robertson (1867–1948), artist and writer.

We may not appreciate now, with the wide realm of pitch-and-toss lying between, that during the mid-1930s a virtual National Theatre – the term never mentioned – was based in St Martin's Lane. There had been much of Gielgud: Noah in André Obey's fantasy which, both as produced by Michel Saint-Denis and as acted, barely shook itself free from an anxious simplicity; the alternation, with Laurence Olivier, of Romeo and Mercutio, and with Gielgud especially, the Queen Mab aria, so subtly spoken ("Her whip of cricket's bone, the lash of film") that it was nearly impossible to replay it in the mind; and a man-of-the-world Trigorin in *The Seagull* (Komisarjevsky's★ production) that was agreeably contentious during the six weeks Gielgud acted it before going with *Hamlet* to America. For a while after this I would almost lose him. Supervening domestic tragedy prevented me from seeing more than the *Richard II* with which he began a four-play season at the Queen's and which – why I have never quite understood – reached me as generally less affecting than the prose *Richard of Bordeaux*. It was a performance, grief's subject and its lord, living in an upper air of its own, divorced from other people in the play. Possibly a year later, and incredulously, I saw Gielgud again, now in a modern comedy, Dodie Smith's *Dear Octopus*. For about nine months he had little to do but be charming, to a Terry second nature. During the last act, surrounded by the best company on the London stage, including the alarming Marie Tempest,† he delivered an after-dinner speech christened Grand Toast.

The Lyceum *Hamlet*, a grander toast to English acting, brought Gielgud back to himself; but John Worthing in *The Importance of Being Earnest* aside, high comedy of the blood royal, a revenant, gloriously in key, from the St James's of the 1890s, some of Gielgud's work – I could not see it all – was more distant than it had been, technically exact yet maybe less instantly communicable. An exception was the Old Vic *Lear* of 1940. This did bring an extraordinary emotional thrust to the fever-chills of the hovel and to the ultimate quintuple "Never," more Gielgud's creation,

★ Theodore Komisarjevsky (1882–1954), Russian-born director who came to England in 1919 and exerted a considerable influence on European theatre.

† Dame Marie Tempest (1864–1942), actress who specialises in light comedy.

I believed, than that of his mentor, Harley Granville-Barker,★ about whom so much would be said. The old man was like a Dartmoor church that they called in the seventeenth century "full bleak and weather-beaten, all alone as it were forsaken". But from ensuing years, the decade of the 1940s, I do recall, for various reasons, less than I should: Dearth in J. M. Barrie's *Dear Brutus* where memories of du Maurier's uncanny naturalism still reigned; the speaking, rather than the physical drive, of Macbeth where the verse fell in flake upon flake of fire that smouldered at length to the embers of Dunsinane; Clive in Maugham's *The Circle*, mercilessly prim, and summoning; Congreve's Lord Froth, "There's nothing more unbecoming in a man of quality than to laugh"; and his fourth Hamlet (at the Haymarket), possibly an older Hamlet, not a better. After two years' absence in America, Gielgud came home in a pleasant period comedy, *The Return of the Prodigal*, chosen, we can be certain, for its title and disparaged woefully by a generation of critics unaware of St John Hankin.† The prodigal returned genuinely during the early summer of 1949. Then in Christopher Fry's *The Lady's Not For Burning*, the English verse play so glowingly and wittily reborn, Gielgud's was the voice for such phrases as "The involving ivy, the briar,/The convolutions of convolvulus" and "The great grey/Main of moonlight, washing over/The little oyster-shell of this month of April."

Thence across the years with only an infrequent lapse, generally an unfortunate choice of play, though once or twice a dogmatic director had blundered, Gielgud would govern as in the past, adjusting to the movements of a chameleon-stage and never telling us, as some older men would, that the theatre went into irreversible decline during 1930 or, at latest, 1940 ("We can't hear them; we don't understand them," a celebrated actor said to me, momentarily dropping his defences).

Gielgud's name as producer, or director, had become familiar on programmes from Shakespeare to Congreve, Wilde and Chekhov, and even *Charley's Aunt* – once in his youth he had had to cope with Charley Wykeham – but this was his secondary life. It is the actor, the man within the character, we think of first, and undoubtedly when we go back to that majestic Stratford-

★ Harley Granville-Barker (1877–1946), dramatist, director and critic, one of the most influential theatrical figures of the twentieth century.

† St John Hankin (1869–1909), dramatist and parodist.

upon-Avon season of 1950 and a gossip-writer surprising us with the considered verdict: "There are signs of a swing towards Shakespeare." No one would have contradicted him. Gielgud was, piercingly, Angelo, the precisian of *Measure for Measure* whose blood was very snow-broth and who made his first entrance between the cressets, a fanatic with a worm in the brain; Benedick (his own production), all light and life; Cassius, in whose bitter tones the flood of Tiber was chafing with its shores; and Lear, less arresting than he had been during 1940 but often sovereign, as in the sharp twist of the lip at the third repetition of the name before the curse: "O Lear, Lear, Lear!/Beat at this gate, that let thy folly in." I may slide forward, dropping a regretful sigh, to a final *Lear*, Japanese-designed (Palace, 1955).* There, among the night's alarms, the King wore around his face a vast drooping circlet of white horsehair, and on his head what looked like an inverted hatstand. (Victor Cookman, of *The Times*, whispered during the interval, "How can any man be so patient!") That was thirty years ago. Gielgud has not suffered from other efforts to "find a setting and costumes which would be free of historical and decorative association".

Today in my diary, lines spoken by him, and not only from a noble Shakespearean programme, *The Ages of Man*, have become a personal anthology. I cannot hope to find again a comparable cry for Leontes in the last act of *The Winter's Tale* – so direct after the earliest gnarled and knotted verse – "Stars, stars, and all eyes else dead coals!" Somebody complained with reason that I had quoted this three times in as many weeks. At the close of Peter Brook's production of *The Tempest*, there was the revelation, "Behold, Sir King, the wronged Duke of Milan, Prospero" in a voice that filled Drury Lane as an autumn night's high tide takes a Cornish beach. In *Henry VIII*, on the Old Vic stage we had Wolsey falling from the world like "a bright exhalation in the evening". These things one expected; but one could not have expected, from Coward's comedy, *Nude with Violin*, to recall the suave valet's sudden "Search me!" Not perhaps an epigram but uttered with such a beautifully judged pause between the words that it reached us like a rocket of wit.

That piece, whatever we may have thought of it, did run; but there were gaps when Gielgud could not find a plausible part.

* A production designed by Isamu Noguchi (b. 1904), Los Angeles-born Japanese sculptor and designer. Associated with the Martha Graham ballet.

Though Enid Bagnold was a dear woman, verbally and technically most elegant, her Ferdinand in *The Last Joke*, a Romanian prince ("shaken with the gaiety of inscrutable jokes or with unheralded furies") and a higher mathematician into the bargain, was hardly meant for the Gielgud who, years before, had directed *The Chalk Garden*. He had to be a capriciously untheatrical Caesar in a version of Thornton Wilder's epistolary novel, *The Ides of March*, even if all Rome could rise in the enunciation of "Capitol" and "Palatine". I cannot feel that, from Peter Shaffer's *The Battle of Shrivings*, he ever ponders now on the trials of a philosophic humanist–pacifist during a play that, like Pinero's lark pie, was "architecturally disproportionate". And in Shaw's *Caesar and Cleopatra*, at Chichester, he was never intended to be a Caesar in the child Queen's nursery equipped with slides and hoops and space-hoppers.

Even so, he has always been ready to expend his imagination, loyalty, extreme intelligence, voice, and wit. A classical actor, he has kept off Ibsen, though I have wondered sometimes what he might have done as Julian in any speakable conflation of *Emperor and Galilean*. Chekhov he has loved since the beginning. We know how sympathetically he played Gaev, ineffectual brother in *The Cherry Orchard*, who covers embarrassment by muttering the jargon of the billiards-table, babbling of green baize, or apostrophising the bookcase; and how in Ivanov he discovered an authority that in anyone else would have been amazing, for the fatigued landowner, a person uncommonly like Edward Lear's "old man at a junction whose feelings were wrung with compunction".

During the 1960s John Gielgud, keeping pace with history, began excitingly to play himself into the newest theatre. He started gently, using an eloquent understatement as the Headmaster ("I am all for free expression if it is rigidly under control") in the school of Alan Bennett's *Forty Years On*, for ever England. More memorably, at the dying fall of David Storey's *Home* (Royal Court) in which we had recognised slowly what kind of home it must be, he was intensely affecting and dignified as, with Ralph Richardson, he held the play's broken rhythms, its elliptical, unconcentrated dialogue, and at the last peered from the terrace into the darkening sky and his darkening life. Only now and again the mask had dropped and the tears flowed; I had not known anyone perform more quietly and movingly than Gielgud did. At the same theatre, in Charles Wood's *Veterans*, with John Mills beside him, he shifted to self-parody in the grand manner as a knighted actor, a first figure of the stage but not as yet beyond a footnote in the cinema. Doomed to fragmentary drama at the heart of film chaos, Sir Geoffrey gallantly decorated an Imperial epic set somewhere in Turkey. All of this was happier than a third Court play, Edward Bond's *Bingo*. Gielgud had been acting Prospero at the Old Vic/National where he had resembled some Jacobean magus ten years beyond man's life. Now he had to face with his incorrigible nobility and not worrying about any Droeshout or Janssen likeness, a personage named Shakespeare, doomed "to point the relationship between any writer and his society". Rather, in Gielgud's presence, he was a man who could have written the First Folio.

Richer again, most permanent of his new-stream parts, was a seedy, sandalled, lank-haired hanger-on in *No Man's Land*, at the National. Unrecognisable if it were not for the first-violin voice, this egregious Spooner found himself alternately humble and arrogant on an August night at a house in Hampstead (owner, Ralph Richardson; dramatist, Harold Pinter). The meaning we could argue for ourselves; we have not forgotten Gielgud's transformation.

There, then, it is. We have reached the eightieth birthday of a great actor who has kept faith with the past but who has not loitered in the backward and abysm of time: a Hamlet and Lear who has been also, let us say, the abstracted father ("Perhaps it has been dull for you – how could it be otherwise?") in the television script of *Brideshead Revisited*. I think of a spring morning in one of the foyers of the National Theatre, the launching of Professor Eric Salmon's book on Harley Granville-Barker. For twenty minutes, entirely relaxed, talking without a note and slipping easily over forty and fifty years, his voice flashed, swayed, flickered in silver just as it was doing on that futile June night in 1928. Tragical-comical-historical-pastoral, scene undividable or poem unlimited: Hamlet (which he has played more than 500 times), Lear, Oedipus, Richard II, Benedick, Leontes, Macbeth, Oberon, Valentine (*Love for Love*), Angelo, Ivanov, Gaev, John Worthing, Spooner, Sir Geoffrey: so much, and more, that endures in the living progress of the twentieth-century theatre. Listening to him in the mind at this period of happy returns (our Grand Toast) we see constantly, as he has said in another context, the whole span of the arc, the beginning, middle, and end:

> Now let the seasons rest. Have we not heard
> Th'unclouded summer of the English word?

I am sure that, for Sir John Gielgud in the theatre, it must always be high summer.

# ANGUS
# McBEAN

## ANGUS McBEAN

Any illustrated record of the theatre of the 1940s and 1950s will inevitably contain photographs by Angus McBean (b. 1904). For almost two decades he was the foremost theatrical photographer of the day. Most West End plays, especially those presented by H. M. Tennent Ltd., were recorded by his camera. All the leading actors and actresses sat for him, but he first crossed Gielgud's path long before he focused on him through a view-finder.

# ANGUS McBEAN

When I was eighteen (I am exactly the same age as John) and it was 1922, my father died and I was able to throw up my job as a bank clerk and come to London in search of culture and art. I tried to find them as a shop assistant in Liberty's. I suppose in first the antique department and afterwards in the interior-decorating section I learned a lot, but it was not enough and I started to go nightly to the galleries of London theatres: I remember even sitting in complete dazed incomprehension through *The Ring* at Covent Garden. Anna Pavlova, I found, was much easier and then came the historic 1926 season with Komisarjevsky producing at the tiny theatre at Barnes.

The notices were ecstatic, especially for one John Gielgud, of whom, I must admit, I had never heard before. So on the third night I made the endless peregrination to Barnes and thereafter almost every night. I was hooked: here I thought I could see a kind of greatness – perhaps I was right.

The first time I ever came into professional contact with John was in 1933 when he produced and played the name part in *Richard of Bordeaux*. I had got to know the three remarkable ladies who did stage designing under the name of Motley.* They were quite new at the job and wanted a huge false proscenium made to stand permanently at each side of the stage, so I built it in their studio which was just opposite the New Theatre in St Martin's

* Sophie Harris (1901–66), Margaret Harris (b. 1904) and Elizabeth Montgomery (b. 1902).

Lane. It was an enormous job – they were huge, the full height of the stage and five feet wide. Motley had drawn them: medieval French townscapes with a kind of false perspective like the drawings in the Duc de Berry's *Book of Hours*. I knew nothing about building stage scenery, but I had just lost my job with Liberty's and would have undertaken anything. I built them of wood and tin, then Motley painted them; they weighed tons and how they passed the fire test, I shall never know.

John Gielgud was fascinated and came almost every day to see progress and I got to know him quite well. Then came the day when the Motleys were bellyaching as to how they were to get all the medieval shoes for the rather large cast made: I who had never made a shoe, said, "Oh, I can make them." So I went backstage at the New and ran a pencil round everyone's feet in the cast – I have still got the ones of John's somewhere.

So, the scenery finished, I went home to work. The Motleys had given me some heavy, stiff canvas, and with my mother's antique Singer sewing machine (which I still have and use), I stitched away at shoe after shoe while my friend Neville Usher piled coat after coat of enamel on them to stiffen them up. Some, especially John's, were very elaborate I remember, the toes curling up and strapping to his knees. My press-cutting books still start with my first London programme proudly stating "Shoes by Angus McBean."

But my first meeting with John Gielgud must have been before this. Every year I used to go to the Old Vic Ball which was usually on the stage at the Lyceum, as I remember it. It was mainly to dress up, which I have always loved, and one year, having won the first prize for my costume, I found that John was giving away the prizes and heard that extraordinary, idiosyncratic and quite beautiful voice saying, "What an extraordinary costume – but, dear boy, I'm deeply embarrassed to have to give you this." This was a set of records of him orating Shakespeare's most famous soliloquies: heavy, twelve-inch, single-sided 78s; to me the greatest joy.

When I sat down to write this I thought it would be easy, but I soon realised that, in spite of having a close connection with him for most of my career as a stage photographer, I hardly know him as a person at all. After all, the photographer is just someone who is called in, like the plumber, to do a job and to most actors a very boring one too. Only the Stage can really know the Stage. But now, after the event, it's only the fading photographs which remain to show what those famous productions looked like. What John could look like, one week as the romantic Thomas Mendip and next as the ancient Noah!

John was wonderful to photograph, seldom with the elaborate make-ups that Olivier was so brilliant at. He has many more subtleties of expression; though looking through the hundreds of photographs I have taken of him very few are smiling. Perhaps drama was his strong suit or perhaps I took him in very few jolly roles.

I find that the first time I actually photographed a play in which he appeared was the H. M. Tennent production of *The Importance of Being Earnest* which he directed at the Globe Theatre in 1939 and here met Edith Evans, who made Lady Bracknell impossible for any other actress for many years, and also Gwen Ffrangcon-Davies* – but the whole point of this, perhaps the funniest play in the British language, is that the characters themselves are deadly serious.

But before this I had practically forced my way into the Lyceum to photograph his Elsinore Hamlet – just a couple of big heads in the corner of the stage, uncommissioned and unpaid and how proud of them I was. And so on through all those Old Vic, Stratford and H. M. Tennent seasons (for which I was not always the only photographer, as I was for the Oliviers). John was always experimenting; new designers, new photographers, yet he always came back to me.

The last play I photographed at the National, practically the last play I ever photographed, was *Tartuffe* with John as Orgon in 1967 when the National was still at the Old Vic – a rather sad occasion. I found I was expected to shoot in action at a dress rehearsal with ordinary stage lighting. Impossible for my kind of photography and somehow I feel a production Sir John would be quite happy to forget.

It has been a wonderful time and I have been privileged to be photographing the theatre for thirty golden years, years with very great actors, Sir Ralph, Sir Laurence and Sir John and many others. I wonder which of them has given me the most pleasure, which the best pictures? They are so different in style and scope. It would be invidious to make any choice.

* Gwen Ffrangcon-Davies (b. 1891) played opposite Gielgud in *Richard of Bordeaux*, *The Potting Shed* and his 1942 *Macbeth*.

Which brings me to one last memory – to October 1935 when I was feeling hard up and fed up. It was raining and a Saturday. "I'll go and have a cup of tea with the Motleys," I said to myself. Up the long iron fire-escape to their wonderful studio in a yard just opposite the New Theatre, a huge whitewashed room said to have been Chippendale's workshop.

Well, the Motleys were away and there was obviously to be no tea. George Devine★ who had just come to work for them was there and a hunched-up young man in a macintosh by the gas fire to whom I suppose I was introduced. I always thought that George didn't like me much though later he did employ me, but he said, making conversation, "Have you seen our play yet?" "No," said I, realising he was referring to *Romeo and Juliet* at the New Theatre opposite, for which Motley had done the decoration. Now John Gielgud was producing and he had elected to play Mercutio for the first fortnight, giving Romeo to Laurence Olivier for the opening, and I went on to say that I was waiting for Olivier to leave Romeo and for John to take over . . . Whereupon the young man by the fire shot to his feet and said, "Well I'd better get back for the curtain. Bye."

We stood in stunned silence for a moment; then I said, "My God, that was Olivier."

"Not your afternoon, Angus," said George.

Why Larry ever forgave me I shall never know. At any rate I suppose he couldn't have thought I would have been deliberately so gratuitously rude and he sent me two very grand seats, following a crawling letter from me. I can't say which was the best as they were so different, but I have always been swept away by John's delivery of Shakespeare's words.

★ George Devine (1910–1966), a founder director of the English Stage Company (at the Royal Court from 1956). Originally an actor. He was married to one of the Motleys, Sophie Harris.

# EMLYN
# WILLIAMS

# EMLYN WILLIAMS

Of all the contributors to this book, Emlyn Williams (b. 1905) was the first to see Gielgud on the stage. Since then they have been close friends and colleagues. Williams's plays include *Spring 1600* (1934), *He Was Born Gay* (1937) – both directed by Gielgud – *Night Must Fall* (1935) and *The Corn is Green* (1938). He is renowned for his one-man performances of Charles Dickens and Dylan Thomas, and is the author of two outstanding volumes of memoirs, *George* (1961) and *Emlyn* (1973).

# EMLYN WILLIAMS

On Monday evening, January 28th, 1924, when I was an undergraduate of eighteen and a bit, I sat in the Oxford Playhouse, then a flimsy sketchily converted building in the Woodstock Road. I was in my weekly (creaky) kitchen chair for the first night of Congreve's *Love for Love*. It was also the first appearance of a newcomer to the company. *Valentine . . .* JOHN GIELGUD.

Not knowing the play, I visualised him as a seasoned old character actor, fortyish. A woman behind me looked up from her programme and whispered, "Poor man, how does he pronounce it, *Jeel*-gud?" It did look outlandish. Not a good stage name, I thought. As bad, in its way, as *Coward*. (John was to tell me, much later, that during his first job, on tour, the local paper had announced that "the small part of the messenger was adequately portrayed by Joan Gillseed . . .")

The curtains parted to reveal Valentine seated at a table, reading, and Jeel-gud turned out to be young (not yet twenty) and very striking in a long curly wig. He motioned languidly to his servant, "Jeremy, take this book away. I'll take a turn and digest what I've read."

To begin with, the usual creaking; but once he got going, in his first leading part, all nose and passion and dragging calves and unbridled oboe of a voice – how nervous he must have been – the creaking stopped. It was all a little large for the hall, but the tall haughty creature held the stage all right, and went mad with a will. Later in the week, *Isis* couldn't get his name right either. "A very interesting performance by Mr Gielgerd."

I was never out of the clubrooms of the OUDS (the Oxford University Dramatic Society) so could hardly miss Gielgud's occasional visits in between the gruelling rehearsals which I envied him so keenly; he would blow in with the President or somebody else important. I would sit in a corner behind a copy of *Variety*.

He was, of course, a contemporary of all of us, but seemed years older. This was partly because he was a working actor, and a leading one, but there was more to it than that. We would have been horrified to be asked to admit it, but the truth was that we were all boys, while he was a grown-up – indeed, it was impossible to imagine that he had ever been an adolescent. Each of us, like most undergraduates, was studiedly playing the *part* of a grown-up (the exception being an elfin mischievous freak of a fourth-former with a protruding tooth and another handicap of a name, Betjeman), while the real-life actor among us, the same age, was effortlessly and naturally mature. And unselfconscious. And fluent. It was soon clear, to any eavesdropper, that many doors were closed to him – moreover, closed *by* him – and then locked with a key to be thrown away: the doors to politics, science, religion, sport, family life. Indeed, he needed no doors: his world was the Theatre, where he stood foursquare amid scenery, with in his ears his beloved music, fearlessly facing, across the footlights, the audience which was his inherited destiny.

Then, just as you were envying the poise and the swift unequivocal judgment – on Ibsen, Shakespearean obscurities, Purcell's theatre music, Shaw's impending *Saint Joan*, Edith Evans' Millamant, Stanislavsky – with every comment irradiated by a passionate interest in people and things which made his conversation quite free from self-display; just as you sat increasingly in awe of the imperious turn of the head, the pundit would toss into the air some appetising morsel of trivial West End gossip, embellished with some atrociously risqué pun – "This girl Tallulah is *too* much, in *The Dancers* apparently she wears not a stitch underneath, a case of no-drawers makes you a draw I suppose, no beating about the bush when *she* does a high kick" – and then a shrill cackle utterly at variance with the other personality.

The callow circle round him was determined not to be taken aback, but it was an effort. It certainly made this strange creature more than just impressive. He was fun.

To jump ahead. Years later, a friend told me of an example of John's absorption in the theatre, which cropped up quite unexpectedly. The two of them, playing in the same film, were sitting on the set in their canvas chairs, whiling away one of the long waits; John was reading. The other, wrestling with his *Times* crossword, leant over, "Sorry, but is there a character in Shakespeare called the Earl of Westmoreland?"

"Yes," John answered, without looking up, "in *Henry IV Part Two*." Then, to break the bad news, he turned to my friend. "But it's a very poor part." And went back to his book.

★   ★   ★

After Oxford, nine years passed – not so many, but we were at the age when nine seemed like twenty-nine. Ih 1933, while playing in New York I wrote *Spring, 1600*, a costume play calling for brilliant direction. While doing so, I read with envy of "GIELGUD'S TRIUMPH," after years of slogging at the Old Vic, as the West End star and director of *Richard of Bordeaux*. He had arrived. Returning to London, I was greeted with the unbelievable news that he had read my play and wanted to direct it.

I rang him. "I love your play, do come round tomorrow, eleven thirty, 7 Upper St Martin's Lane, goodbye." He had spoken so quickly I could barely understand him. After New York, he had sounded like a melodious machine-gun.

On my way I stopped outside the New Theatre. RICHARD OF BORDEAUX JOHN GIELGUD. Along the side and round the corner, the pit-stools for the matinée. I studied the large photographs of Richard. With the crown set on the long blond hair, the robes flowing, the etched mouth sensitive and fired with the defiance of spoilt youth, the nobly androgynous figure struck a new note in the theatre.

I climbed steep narrow stairs to a top flat. In the interim I had only rarely met my host in restaurants or at parties: it was a nodding acquaintance and I was in awe of him. I visualised an impeccable drawing room with one good painting, a classical bust and lofty talk about costume drama with a couple of reverent acolytes hovering.

The door was opened by my old friend Richard Clowes; I was relieved, he would ease my visit. Music, from a fine gramophone, I guessed Bach. The severe beat of phrase after disciplined phrase was a little chilling, and prepared me for the impeccable room.

It was nothing of the sort, being unpretentiously small with good furniture and family pictures and comfortably lived in by bachelors with many books and scripts. Dick introduced me to John Perry, who shared the flat: he was a tall young man, gauntly handsome with thinning hair and a mocking manner which contrived to hide a kind heart. Dick asked if John G. was still asleep.

"He's in the bathroom massaging the old temples. I keep telling him it's no use playing Canute, we'll both be bald by forty."

The phone rang. John P. answered it and called, "Get your roller-skates on, it's Basil Dean!" It was like being in digs on tour. Except that Basil Dean was London's leading director. Gielgud hurried in, bare-legged and with the familiar dragging stride. The shabby old dressing-gown suggested a toga, the white lathered cheeks the beard of a senator and the shaving brush a sliver of papyrus. Yes, the twenty-nine-year-old hair was receding.

"Sorry, Basil, I was shaving . . ." Behind the musical machine-gun, a nervous deference. "Very kind of you but if all goes well I'll be directing the new Maugham, thank you very much. Goodbye." He hung up, strode to the door and turned. "When I remember how beastly he was to me when I took over from Noël in *The Constant Nymph*. Emlyn, how nice to see you again," giving a quick smile as he shook hands with me as if he were fully dressed in a restaurant. "Did you love America? Dean called it an understudy performance and you should have heard the smarminess just now. It's a mad world, me masters!"

A giggle of pleasure, unexpected and high-pitched – I remembered it from years back – and he was gone. Bach tinkled into silence. John P. prepared coffee, I looked at a book, Dick read the papers. John G. returned from the bedroom, elegant from head to foot in a light spring suit. (During all the years ahead, I was never to see him other than flawlessly and unobtrusively dressed, with a figure as slimly correct in his eighth decade as it has been since eighteen.) He put on the other side of Bach, sat back in an armchair, closed his eyes with a sigh and looked completely exhausted. "Oh dear . . ."

I thought the conversation might now take a more elevated turn, and was glad it did not. John P. said, "We've been touching on the hair situation."

"Don't. In modern plays I'm only happy in a hat. Why can't men lunch out with their heads covered, like women can? The women *have* their hair, it's the men who need the hats. I mean look at Dickie here; his widow's peak is practically in his glasses. It isn't fair."

"Pray continue," Dick said, "you make me sound irresistible. God took one look at me and said, 'Must compensate for all that. We'll take the hair away from the beautiful ones and give it to this poor old thing.' "

John G. gave a quick look at my forehead. "You're lucky too – just like Dick!"

John P. caught my eye and gave a delighted laugh. "Things that could be better put, you'll get used to it." In most people there exists, between mind and tongue, a brake which swiftly advises rephrasing or even "Don't say it at all". The Gielgud brake was missing.

"They say thin hair means you're brainy. I wonder if one *could* get away with putting 'To be or not to be' before the scene with the Players? I'd love to try it. I may be losing my hair but that was the seventh offer since yesterday morning. Isn't it marvellous?"

"Marvellous," John P. murmured, "so long as you aren't losing your head as well."

The other John sighed again. "Must remember to tell Jimmy to order three hundred more postcards; after the show I sit signing them in my costume as people come round. Yes, John, I know it's vulgar but I can't resist it: I'm a star!"

After the crow of an excited child, he sat back and closed his eyes. Dick turned a page of his newspaper. "Good notice for last night's play in Auntie *Times*. Didn't you see a run-through?"

When the answer came, the pale fastidious Roman profile was as perfectly married to the music as it was divorced from the words. "Yes I did. It was piss, oh dear . . ."

He again looked exhausted. I was soon to understand that it was a physical attitude as habitual as it was deceptive. He was never tired, had a constitution composed of a million tough wires, and "Oh dear" meant that the mind was wheeling like a kestrel about to pounce, direction unpredictable.

"And so badly acted. Do you like Bach or hate it?" The head bobbed up and the young death-mask jerked back into life. "Dick, don't you think this passage would make a thrilling background for a very cold-blooded *Duchess of Malfi* murder?"

He talked. Out of the machine-gun, interspersed with the schoolboy puns, the names followed one another like grapeshot. I almost needed footnotes. "The girls" were the firm of Motley, the three brilliant young designers he had discovered for *Richard of Bordeaux*, and "Bronnie" was his presenter, Bronson Albery. He addressed himself to me, with effortless courtesy.

"The girls would do *Malfi* marvellously and so cheaply. Have you seen *Mata Hari*, Garbo? I wept buckets but then I cry at everything. John says the tears start when I see the censor's certificate. D'you know anything about the new Cagney film? When was *Malfi* last done?"

And without warning, the eyes fixed me like a searchlight. "I loved your play, how d'you feel about the last act? But there's so much to the rest. Peggy for the girl, d'you think, or Jessica or Celia? What about Edna? She was beastly to me too in *The Nymph* but she has quality. Then there's Angela, she wouldn't play it Baddeley but Edna might be Best" – a shrill cackle, then the director again – "I'll show it to Bronnie when we've got the last act right; you've done it so well . . ."

I left to the pulsating strains of Mozart. The passers-by in St Martin's Lane looked dull.

Two days later, a morning session at the flat, just the two of us. We went through the first act of my *Spring, 1600* in detail. He had made a close study and produced suggestion after suggestion, each bringing the script to stage life imaginatively and yet realistically. "I've got it – suppose we start the music in the house here, instead of in the garden, then we could move the action over there . . ." It was bracing.

In between my stint at Gaumont-British Studios, where I was under contract as actor and writer, the sessions continued. Down-to-earth tidying and shaping. "Why shouldn't *she* have the line instead? Much funnier – no, I've got a still better idea . . ." Then a special morning devoted to Act Three. He felt that Lady Coperario was such a colourful character – "whores always are; let's call the play *Whores for Tennis*" – that she must carry on into the last scene.

"Then Isabel Jeans *might* consider it. Perhaps a scene in her palatial lodgings, with a couple of dabs of paint the Motleys would make them look like gorgeous Tiepolo draperies, a rostrum on wheels perhaps, Burbage drunk on her bed, panic in his theatre . . ." He made it sound thrilling. Every time I hear Bach or Mozart on the radio, I think of those mornings.

By August the last act was back from the typist and in the hands of Bronson Albery. "Emlyn, I have a feeling he'll like it now the last act is stronger but you never know with him: Bronnie soit qui mal y pense. What about Ralph for Burbage? Not romantic enough though a beard could work wonders . . ."

*Richard of Bordeaux* being in its seventh month, its star was given two weeks' holiday, "to make a break", took a suite at the Royal Crescent, Brighton, littered it with scripts, and asked me and Dick Clowes down for a couple of days. He went for walks between us along the front, the ozone fertilising his mind with ideas while his eyes spotted theatre faces with the excitement of a gallery first-nighter. "I've got rather a good idea for *The Dream* – look, there's Binnie Hale! – to do it nude, or as near as one could go – wouldn't it be superb!"

He made it sound just that, till he added, "With everybody starkers we could just call it *Bottom*", and shrieked with nursery laughter. Back in the suite, while Dick and I sat on the balcony reading, he would emerge holding his shaving brush.

"Dickie, we could offer the ham–old–actor part in *Spring* to Frederick Volpe. Is he dead?"

"Yes."

"Oh. Then we couldn't." Exit.

Another time he would glance disdainfully down at Dick's newspaper. "I don't like Ramsay MacDonald's face; is he a good Prime Minister?" and was gone. Dick said, "The nearest John's ever got to politics is the plot of *Julius Caesar*."

One rainy afternoon he decided on a night out in London. By now I knew him well enough to know that he would take us to a theatre, but not well enough to know which one.

After a fine early dinner at the Café Royal, Dick and I found ourselves sitting in the front of a stage box, with the holiday-maker lurking behind us in the shadows. We were at the New Theatre, watching *Richard of Bordeaux*. "I'm curious to see it from the front." As the theatre darkened Dick whispered to me, "Would you call *this* 'making a break'?"

Glen Byam Shaw★ was playing Richard prior to touring in the part, and playing well. At the end of one emotional scene between the king and his wife, I stole a look behind me: John was not just moved, he was weeping. I was in the company of a child playing with double mirrors. When at the end we hurried through the pass-door, the stagehands stacking scenery looked through the visitor without recognising him. They had plainly never seen him in a suit.

Glen was staggered – "thank God I didn't know" – and delighted by praise generous and sincere. Then John took me and Dick out to supper, as if after a first night he had enjoyed. Dick said, "John dear, I know the play moved you, but I did once see you lean forward and count the house through your tears."

"Dickie Clowes, that's a wicked thing to say. Actually it wasn't at all bad, I was surprised . . ."

Weeks passed, more work, then suddenly the green light, all was set. Casting meant fevered mornings at Number 7, with the Gielgud mind wheeling and pouncing. The problem was the girl, a star part. "Jessie Tandy's in the Ackland play, Peggy, if you can believe it, is going into that musical farrago at the Coliseum. Who does she think she is, Phyllis Dare? Angela's on tour with Glen. Who on earth can we get? Oh dear . . ." The king sat back, sick unto death.

But the next day the *Daily Mirror* displayed a picture of Edna Best, back from Hollywood. The king revived. "But she looks sixteen! . . . Marvellous pathos and comedy and I rather enjoy the thought of employing somebody who's been rude to me. Where's she staying?"

Dick said, "She'll never say yes . . ."

But she did, appeared at the first reading, and made an exciting impression. Next morning, on stage, John read a note from her: she suddenly had to leave for the States. The whole cast was standing around but John was too concerned to care. "It's Bart of course . . ." (Herbert Marshall, Miss Best's husband) "I did hear he's been a bit footloose in Hollywood." It was not the happiest way to describe a glamorous film star who happened to be one-legged, but only Dick and I noticed.

★ Glen Byam Shaw (b. 1904) actor, and later director. Director of the Shakespeare Memorial Theatre at Stratford-upon-Avon in the 1950s. Married to Angela Baddeley (1904–76).

Somebody called out "Madeleine Carroll!" "No," John said. "She's like Emlyn, at the beck and call of that ghastly Gaumont-British . . ."

Joyce Bland was the final choice: a fine actress but not a star. Day after day, Dick and I sat and watched the play lurch and grow under the feverish, merciless care of its director; nobody could have guessed that he was playing an arduous part eight times a week; he was tireless.

The first big day came when he took the play straight through, scene by scene. After a back-breaking five hours, an incident which was to amuse Dick for a long time. John was sitting in front of us, pale as wax and strong as steel, holding the megaphone through which – to save his voice for the evening and pacify Bronnie – he would marshal the front-of-cloth rabble (all the subsidiary cast) through their paces. Just as the scene got under way, a noise like thunder. "Stop!"

They all obliged, and peered over the footlights. "Sorry, everybody," the director boomed through his artificial aid, "but you're all being too slow. We must get it tearing along at this point. Emlyn agrees with me that from now on his last act is thin."

As the boom died away Dick heard me say, without aid but from the heart, "John, I agree that it's thin, but please *not through a megaphone.*"

"Terribly sorry, how stupid of me, how good-tempered you are, right, everybody, *off.*" The scene turned into a horse race, but whether that helped to fatten up my last act I was not in a state to judge.

Wednesday, January 31st, 1934. It was on me at last. John phoned, "Glad I've got a matinée, take my mind off . . ." Then a bombardment. "I'm happy to have done it whatever happens, you've been so patient, it's a lovely play."

We had a definite *succès d'estime*, which is French for "distinguished failure". John was typically generous, "Too bad, partly my fault, I should have asked you to cut before the first night not after. I still love the play." *Bordeaux* finally closed, and he went into a contemporary piece, *The Maitlands.* "If my public don't see me soon in a pair of trousers, they'll think I haven't got any."

1935. During the run of *Night Must Fall*, John was godfather to our son Alan. "Not really my part, my dears, but I'll have a shot at it . . ."

Then I happened to read a book about the lost Dauphin, the child of Marie Antoinette who disappeared in the Revolution at the age of ten and was never seen again. What happened to him? I wrote a play, for John, on the premise that the child had survived, in England, as an anonymous young music master in a country house. Comes Waterloo, which makes him Louis XVII of France. An emissary of Louis XVIII arrives, and convinces the rightful king that his only way out is suicide. It was an excitingly promising idea which somehow went wrong in the cooking, the ingredients being an uneasy mixture of drama (melodrama?) flavoured with poetic prose ("fine writing"), period comedy and high farce.

Moreover, at the first night, a salient fault became immediately obvious. I had constructed the play as the unfolding of a mystery: gradually the insignificant music master is made conscious of his heritage, and is, step by step, incredibly transformed into the King of France. It was to be a story with the suspense which has to be at the core of any effective play or film, whether drama or comedy.

John's first entrance, into the grand drawing room, was by an unobtrusive door, downstage, leading to the kitchen quarters, as a flustered young nobody. "I'm so sorry, I thought this was the linen-cupboard . . ." Well, on the first night there emerged, to great applause, *not* a shy underling from below stairs, with no idea of future developments, but the King of France; John was fresh from a triumph, in London and New York, as Hamlet, and the nobody wore an invisible crown which could be spotted from the back of the gallery. Here was Hamlet again, Prince of Pantries, and the plot of the play was instantly given away. In a part written for him, the actor was miscast!

To do with the same play, a startlingly ironical development may be noted, wryly. I had, very early on, hit on a beautifully appropriate title; everybody else liked it too. It is on record that when Marie Antoinette first set eyes on her baby son, she remarked on the mischievous half-smile on his face and happily spoke . . . four words most poignant in view of the child's future. And the four words became my title.

But this was as far back as 1937. On television in America, I am sometimes asked if I have worked with Sir John Gielgud, and the first time this happened, I spoke of course of *Spring, 1600*. "Did you work with him again?" "Oh yes, three years later, in a play of mine called . . ." Then amnesia set in, I just couldn't remember the name of it. Because what Marie Antoinette said was "*Il est né gai*". So I had called the play *He Was Born Gay*. A sad story, and like many sad stories, funny . . .

It so happened that John and I never worked together again. It occurs to me that though neither of our ventures were successful, we never had a cross word and have stayed close friends ever since.

Close enough, indeed, for me to be often asked, "What's he *really* like?" Which of us can succinctly answer that question about anybody, however intimate seems our knowledge? What I can try to do is to correct the impression he usually makes on the thousands of people who meet him fleetingly. I can hear them, "He's very charming, but . . . sort of distant, frightening almost, oh he has exquisite manners but lays down the law a bit, says what he thinks all right, is he self-centred, is he selfish on the stage? Does he care what other people think? Is he conceited? Most actors are, aren't they?"

Well, most actors aren't, and John is the least conceited of all. And he is no more self-centred than anybody else – where else can we be centred but in ourselves?

The reason for this false image, of course, is that very rare characteristic: complete honesty. "*Says what he thinks . . .*" Of course he talks about himself, but talks just as much about other people; when he gives his opinions it is because he is eager to share them with others and to hear theirs. As I had observed as early as Oxford-time, his world – while being exclusive – is not oppressively so, because his curiosity, about the people and things which interest him, is insatiable. "Tell me, how did it go in Sydney? I loved it at the National though I couldn't take to the music . . ." "I hear he's having a big success in New York. I'm so happy for him after that disappointing year . . ." "I'm worried about her. I know she's miserable with that husband, and it's affecting her work."

And if he feels like praising himself, out it comes: if he thinks poorly of himself, out it comes. And he is the same about others – good or bad, everything comes out. "I do have a good figure, but I am inclined to walk so badly, the critics were quite right . . ." During *Bordeaux* – "Eric Portman? He's a tricky one: the trouble is that he and I are in the same *galère* and he's jealous of me because I've suddenly become a star and he hasn't." (True, it was 1940 before Portman became a film name.) But later in the conversation, one could hear John exclaim, "Oh, I was dreadful in that part, missed the point entirely. I tell you who'd have been marvellous, so much better – Eric!"

"*Is Gielgud selfish on the stage?*" The most telling answer to that is a look at the Gielgud repertory season at the Queen's Theatre in 1937–1938, when he was virtually an actor-manager of the all-powerful eminence of Irving. But instead of surrounding himself with sound self-effacing players who would enhance that eminence, he had the professional generosity – and acumen – to engage artists of the highest calibre: Gwen Ffrangcon-Davies, Peggy Ashcroft, Angela Baddeley, Leon Quartermaine, and even one actor, four years younger than him, who was clearly on the brink of becoming a rival in his own romantic field: Michael Redgrave. That was unselfish. And another fact shows the same magnanimity: his intense admiration for other directors who have at times directed him – Komisarjevsky, Saint-Denis and Granville-Baker.

"*Does he care what people think?*" I can best answer that by recalling a young actor playing a small part in *Bordeaux*, an over-ambitious oaf resenting Gielgud's meteoric success and morbidly looking for slights. Offended by John's apparent imperviousness, as a director, to anything but the job in hand, accompanied by the lofty manner which could sound a bit dictatorial, he decided to behave as badly as he could throughout the run, like a class bully cheeking the art master only a year older than himself. "No, I don't feel like moving over there, I'm staying here, ridiculous suggestion . . ."

Those strangers I have mentioned, visualising John possibly as a brilliantly impervious egotist, would have been startled by his reaction. The calculated insolence of his enemy (because that is what this actor had turned himself into) so distressed him, so preyed on his mind, that it almost got to marring his enjoyment of his success. Often, during our mornings over *Spring, 1600*, his mind would suddenly dart off, "What d'you think he muttered last night, in front of the whole company?" His bewilderment was touching in its defenceless vulnerability. The situation called for ruthless strong-arm tactics which he was too fastidious to try to fall back on. It was illuminating.

"*Has he friends?*" One striking fact about J.G. is his enduring devotion to so many of his leading ladies, as well as to other women friends: Peggy Ashcroft, Angela Baddeley, Diana Wynyard, Margaret Leighton, Vivien Leigh, Molly Keane, Mavis Walker . . . But the most interesting friendship of all is that with another actor – a star at that – which, by the sheer incongruity of the two men, has puzzled onlookers and lasted for nearly half a century: John Gielgud's devotion to Ralph Richardson.

Edith Evans. They were friends of course, but it was a complicated relationship. His admiration for her as an artist amounted to awe, but offstage his feelings were muddied by irritation, for as a person he found her evasive, almost coquettishly so; she resisted his affection. I once told him Sybil Thorndike's comment, Sybil the generous extrovert: "I've always felt whenever I rushed up to Edith in my silly way to say hello, there was a placard round her neck saying '*Keep off the Grass*'!"

"Oh," John said, "that's Edith in a nutshell!" He revered her so much – another proof of his inherent humility – that he would have treasured one word of unstinted praise from her more than from anyone he ever worked with. He longed for it, and it never came. "Once, after one of those special performances when you just *know* you've been at your best, I heard she'd been in front and was thrilled. She came round and I waited. Small-talk, then finally she said 'Well, Johnnie, it was eighty-five per cent right . . .' and that was it. I tried not to mind, but I was furious."

As to his friendship with me, I will only say that I have before me, as I compose this, the long letter John wrote me after my wife died in 1970, in that minuscule hand which called, literally, for a magnifying glass. By the time I had finished reading, the glass was blurred.


After the serious stuff, let us conclude, like the old bulging entertainments, with a divertissement.

Many prominent people become well known for an idiosyncrasy which becomes quoted: the Rev. Spooner has his spoonerisms, Goldwyn his goldwynese. And Gielgud has his gielgudies.

Earlier, I mentioned J. Perry's comment on J.G.'s habit of saying things "that could be better put". As, with the years, these oral slips have become more and gleefully seized upon by friends, their perpetrator is, by now, well aware of them. "Oh dear," he once said to me, "I suppose it's a genius for saying the right thing in the wrong way. I seem in my time to have dropped enough bricks to build a new Wall of China. Well, so long as I don't offend, I don't mind making a fool of myself."

Without intending to, I seem to have made a small collection of the said "bricks". These are for the record.

1. The best-known one, big enough to be called a boulder, happened early in the Gielgud career, at the Ivy Restaurant, where he was the luncheon guest of a prominent playwright of the time who was notoriously dull and garrulous company. Just as there came a pause for breath, a man passed the table. "Thank God he didn't stop," said John, "he's a bigger bore than Eddie Knoblock," and turned back to his host. Who was Eddie Knoblock.

I once asked him if this was a true story, and he confessed that it was.

"But when you said it, what happened?"

"I was embarrassed."

"I should think so. But what did *he* do?"

John reflected. "Mmm . . . Just looked slightly puzzled, and went on boring."

2. In 1933, during the run of *Bordeaux*, he directed *The Merchant of Venice* at the Old Vic. During the rehearsals necessary during his performances at the New, he was helped out by Harcourt Williams, the distinguished veteran actor-director whom he much admired. Nobody could have appreciated the gesture more than John. Came the first night. At the end of his performance at the New, John scrambled out of his clothes and into a taxi, and got to the Old Vic in time for the last curtain. At the end of the calls and the cheers, he joined the actors, beautifully praised and thanked them all, and finished up with "The person to whom I am truly grateful is my friend Harcourt Williams, who has – believe me – done all the donkey-work."

3. The following year John was casting *The Laughing Woman*, a play about a brilliant young sculptor and his mistress. "Bronnie is insisting on Stephen Haggard for the part. He's splendid but *much* too well-bred. It calls for an actor who would convey somebody savage, uncouth – Emlyn, *you* should be playing it!"

4. In 1940, again at the Old Vic, and again a curtain speech, after a performance of *The Tempest*, I was in the audience. It was at one of the darkest moments of the war, invasion seemed imminent and many mothers with American connections had decided to

brave the very real submarine dangers of the Atlantic and set out with their small children. One of their number was Jessica Tandy, who had opened as Miranda, played until she sailed, and then was replaced by Peggy Ashcroft; they were two first-rate young actresses, who, as I indicated earlier, were often in the running for the same part. After this particular performance Prospero stepped forward and held out a hand to stem the applause. "Ladies and gentlemen, I know you will rejoice with all of us, in relief at the news just received – Jessica Tandy is safely in America!"

It seemed to me that for a second Peggy was wondering how to make it clear that she was showing the right kind of relief.

5. The 1950s. On tour with a solo performance as *Charles Dickens*, I was lunching with John in New York. He mentioned that he wasn't sure what he wanted to do next. I said, "Why don't *you* do a one-man show based on Shakespeare? So many parts you could interpret which you could never play in the plays. It would be exciting."

A pause. "Oh no, I think one should keep that sort of thing for one's old age."

I was what I considered a youthful fifty. (Luckily, a year or so later he changed his mind.)

6. A small dinner-party at John's house in 1951 during rehearsals for *The Winter's Tale* with Diana Wynyard. Diana had been delayed at a costume fitting which John was anxious about, and as soon as she arrived we proceeded to the dining table, flawlessly prepared for the party. "Molly dear," said our host to my wife, of whom he was very fond, "you sit over there, and Diana, you sit next to me because I want to talk to you . . ." Molly, Diana and I exchanged a quick look.

7. Washington, 1979. John was in a Pinter play, and on a night off came to my Dylan Thomas performance. At supper afterwards, "I did enjoy my evening, the end is so moving . . ." I waited for the brick, and it came. "Your breath control is so much better, none of that gasping and gulping when you played Richard III at the Vic . . ."

I was silent for a moment. That had been in 1937, forty-two years before. One thing I had always been complimented on, was my "breath control". At the Vic, had I *really* started the evening off with *Now is the winter* – gulp gulp – *of our discontent* – gasp gasp – *made glorious summer* – gulp gulp . . .?

8. In 1969, on one of the few occasions when I was ailing enough
to be confined to my bed, John called to see me, full of affectionate concern, and entertained us both for an hour. Then, out of the
blue, "Must go, my dears, when I visit the sick I always stay too
long. I sat for ages with poor Arthur Macrae, but I was glad I'd
been, he died next day."

He had not been gone two minutes before I was out of bed,
fully dressed and pouring a stiff drink.

And so on. Gielgudies not sufficiently numerous to complete
the Wall of China. But enough, perhaps, to immure a couple of
disobedient nuns.

One story, while not coming under the last heading, is still
another example of a kaleidoscopic mind thinking aloud – blurt-
ing, like a child. 1955, Stratford-upon-Avon. John had just
directed the Oliviers in *Twelfth Night*, and it had been a difficult
time: perhaps through dealing with an over-familiar play and
wondering how to freshen it up, he had vacillated. "Our dear
John," Vivien had said once, "the only consistent thing about
you is that you can be depended on to change your mind every
two minutes. In the duel, if you once again alter the moves for
one of us without alerting the other, somebody's going to get
killed."

The reviews were mixed. Vivien later told me that one night at
supper, Edith Evans' name came up; she had not acted since *The
Dark Is Light Enough* and John said, "She won't admit it, being
Edith, but she's getting restless, like all of us she loves to work."
Then – the darting mind again – "oh dear, I've directed this so
badly, I don't suppose any of you will ever want to work with me
again . . ." A sigh, and a split second. "Except perhaps Edith, at a
pinch . . ."

I wished I'd been there to hear Vivien's peal of affectionate
laughter.

Gielgud and Irving. Sir John and Sir Henry . . . Even if such
comparisons weren't odious, there is no way of attempting one:
all that is left of the great Victorian is a couple of pathetically
muffled gramophone records, while – thanks to the marvels of
mechanical reproduction – the major Gielgud performances are

preserved, in sets of boxes (with lids spelling the name right) which – provided the perfect set is buried safe enough from other scientific marvels we all dread – will last pretty well for ever.

It is sad about Irving. But even if he *had* had access to the same wonderful techniques, and had left records, video-tapes, cassettes, what-have-you – of *The Bells, Hamlet, Becket* . . . Ellen Terry once said he was unique in his versatility; but he wasn't quite as versatile as her grand-nephew.

If Irving had had the same scientific help, future generations would indeed be fascinated to watch him standing on a television screen and speaking the speech beginning *To be, or not to be.* But . . . I recently saw *Arthur*, a film farce starring Dudley Moore. Never, *never* could the mellifluous Irving tones, the voice of the non-permissive last century, later startle posterity by emanating from an aristocratic valet perched on the edge of a bath and looking superciliously down his nose at his naked employer: "I suppose I am now expected to wash your dick . . ." Bury those boxes deep. They will be valuable.

# CHRISTOPHER FRY

# CHRISTOPHER FRY

Immediately after the Second World War, Christopher Fry was hailed as the leading playwright in the English-speaking theatre. Born in 1907, he was first a schoolmaster, actor and director before writing *A Boy with A Cart* in 1938 and, in 1946, *The Lady's Not For Burning* which starred Gielgud and Pamela Brown. His other plays include *Venus Observed* (with Laurence Olivier; 1950), and *The Dark is Light Enough* (with Edith Evans, directed by Peter Brook; 1954). He was awarded the Queen's Gold Medal for Poetry in 1962.

# CHRISTOPHER FRY

Towards the end of 1930 I saw two plays at the Old Vic, *The Tempest* and *Richard II*. How I came to be there I don't remember. I was teaching in a preparatory school in Surrey, my salary £120 a year, so there was little spare cash for trips to London or for theatre tickets, whatever they cost – though a few years earlier I had sat in the Old Vic gallery for sixpence. But in 1930 I believe I was nearer to the stage, or perhaps the strength of the performance and the intentness of my concentration made it seem so. I may have been treated to a seat in the stalls by the school matron, Grace Lawson. About that time she had taken me to hear a debate between Bernard Shaw and G. K. Chesterton, and to see a production of Eliot's *Sweeney Agonistes* in an upstairs room in Soho, so she may well have been responsible for my first seeing Gielgud act.

My knowledge of Shakespeare in performance had gone no further than Sir Frank Benson's* visits to the County Theatre, Bedford. But here was something of a different nature altogether. The words of Prospero were indeed the sound of a magic island. Over the space of fifty-three years I can still hear his voice addressing the elves of hills, brooks, standing lakes and groves. Even such a word as "appertaining" had its own curious mystery as he turned from Miranda and Ferdinand with:

* Sir Frank Benson (1858–1939), archetypal actor-manager. His Shakespearean company toured the English provinces and his actors were proud to be called Old Bensonians.

> . . . I'll to my book;
> For yet, ere supper-time, must I perform
> Much business . . . appertaining.

When I left school in 1926 I felt fairly hopeful of becoming a writer. Two or three poems had been printed in *Public School Verse*, along with work by other schoolboys, B. J. Miles of Uxbridge County School, Bernard Miles (Lord Miles to be) among them; but in the four years that followed I had somehow lost contact with whatever makes for creativity and, though I made occasional efforts to recapture it, a kind of opacity had taken over my mind, and I saw no way of penetrating it. But then on the November day at the Old Vic in 1930 as I listened to the speech of King Richard which opens the fifth scene of Act Five, I felt for a few vivid moments a reassurance that a way might be found:

> I have been studying how I may compare
> This prison where I live unto the world:
> And for because the world is populous,
> And here is not a creature but myself,
> I cannot do it; yet I'll hammer it out.
> My brain I'll prove the female to my soul,
> My soul the father; and these two beget
> A generation of still-breeding thoughts,
> And these same thoughts people this little world,
> In humours like the people of this world . . .

Gielgud gave the words such a generating precision, exploring the thought by revealing the life of the words, that the speech became for me the act of creation itself. I had never known words spoken with such effect before. The voice mapped out the structure of the passage, almost analytically, yet without losing the indwelling music of it. There may have been other times when this delicate balance of sense and sound evaded him – could such a feeling of something new-minted happen again, I wondered – but on this occasion it was there to perfection; and not so long ago when a television programme presented actors of the various generations speaking a soliloquy from *Hamlet*, it seemed to me that, good as many of the others were, he alone was finding the measure which gave both the substance and the resonance of Shakespeare's lines, the fourth dimension of life which is one of the differences between prose and poetry.

Eighteen years after I had sat wide-eared listening to the words of Prospero and Richard he was in correspondence with me about plans for the production of *The Lady's Not For Burning*. It only shows the freakishness of memory that I have no recollection of first meeting him. The earliest surviving letter, written I think in October 1948, though he has merely dated it "Tuesday", speaks of plans well advanced. I know that things went easily and happily from the start, when he warmly agreed that Pamela Brown should play Jennet. I had written the part for her, and the two of them chimed together in and out of the theatre. They each had a relish for the comicalities of life, and neither had any touch of self-importance. In her letters to me Pam would sometimes affectionately refer to him as "the Young Master". And they both continued to work to improve their performances for as long as the play was played. Five months after the opening night John would write to me:

> I had a good afternoon a week or so ago rehearsing the first act, simplifying and freshening. I play all the beginning far more slowly and detachedly and try to get your bombhappy tipsiness . . . Pam and I have also slowed up the opening of the love scene to give a truer feeling of awkwardness and gradual awakening of interest and familiarity.

The spate of his directorial inventiveness was sometimes difficult to check. Ideas came not single spies but in battalions. Changes of moves and emphasis went on all through the preliminary tour, and continued from time to time throughout the run. When rehearsals started the following year, for taking the play to the States, changes began again. Alison Colvil, the stage director, begged me to dissuade him from any more alterations. "I've rubbed holes through the script," she said. I got back to the auditorium and sat behind him. Almost at once he gave a fresh direction to the actors. I tapped him on the shoulder, ready to suggest that he should leave well alone, but he was already saying delightedly, "Oh good, good! It's always better when it's different." He was still having ideas thirty years later about how to do the play. "I do so wish you would get somebody to direct it in modern dress," he wrote to me, "with a cosy but common-

looking parlour, the man in battledress, the girl in Lanvin, and the
mayor in red flannelette and rabbit fur."

This never-diminishing eagerness to learn his craft, as though
he were always at the beginning of his career, still seeing the fun
of it, is in the comment he made after seeing a production of a
Shakespeare play during the run of *The Lady*:

> A very worried over-conscious production . . . one or two
> lovely bits from the comics . . . otherwise most ill-played. A
> great lesson in how not to carry on when speaking verse. I
> learnt a lot, and Nora (Nicholson) and I haven't *moved* our
> hands on the stage since!

So the mastering of new ground (Spooner in *No Man's Land*,
for instance, a week after his sixty-ninth birthday) came naturally. One pity remains: that we haven't been given the Lear of his
maturity. There were indications in the 1955 production, in spite
of the distraction of the costumes, that we have been denied a
great thing.

# ALEC
# GUINNESS

# ALEC GUINNESS

Alec Guinness (b. 1914) is one of the most distinguished English stage and
screen actors of his generation. As a youthful theatregoer and drama student, he
was to be greatly influenced by Gielgud who was later to prove personally
helpful to him. Guinness was awarded the CBE in 1955 and knighted four years
later.

# ALEC GUINNESS

"Come on from the left. No! No! The *other* left! – Oh, someone make him understand! – Why are you so stiff? Why don't you make me laugh?"

The superb tenor voice, like a silver trumpet muffled in silk, kept up a rapid stream of commentary together with wildly contradictory instructions from the stalls, while I fumbled with my little Temple edition of Shakespeare on the bare stage of the New Theatre. It took a whole morning to set a single page of the text.

Gielgud's directions to the actors were interrupted frequently, in full flight, by his calling out to the designers, Sophie and Margaret Harris and Elizabeth Montgomery, the firm of Motley, "Motleys! Motleys! Would it be pretty to have it painted gold? Perhaps not. Oh, don't fidget, Frith Banbury! Alec Guinness, you are gabbling. Banbury, your spear is crooked. Now turn upstage. No, not you. You! Turn the other way. Oh, why can't you all *act*? Get someone to teach you to *act*!"

And so the dreadful morning wore on, with me, at the vulnerable age of twenty, on the verge of tears and acutely aware of other members of the cast of *Hamlet* (Jack Hawkins, Jessica Tandy, Frank Vosper, George Howe, Laura Cowie and George Devine) sitting on benches at the side of the stage, pretending to read their newspapers to hide their embarrassment or perhaps just quaking in their shoes. Later that day George Devine came in for a Gielgud lashing with, "Oh, why is your voice so harsh? It really is quite ugly. Do *do* something about it."

It was my first experience of being "produced" – as we used to call direction in the early thirties – by my actor-hero, benefactor, patron and later good friend, who gave me my first proper chance in the theatre, cherished my barely visible talent and kept me solidly employed for over two years.

In the summer of 1934 I was a student at the Fay Compton School of Dramatic Art and had been awarded, at the annual show, the school prize; a double-columned, minutely printed volume of Shakespeare's *Collected Works*, bound in leatherette and inscribed, in enormous writing, by Fay.

The judges at the school performance had been Gielgud, Jessie Matthews and Ronald Adam. I had been at the Fay Compton for about seven months, on a scholarship which carried no money, and I was kept from starvation by the gift of jam sandwiches and fruit generously provided by fellow students and a weekly blow-out, given by an old advertising copywriter friend at the Charing Cross Lyons Corner House. I lived on less than thirty shillings a week in a squalid little room off Westbourne Road, allowing myself sixpence a week for a gallery seat at the Old Vic. Walking everywhere, often carrying my shoes to save shoe-leather, I was remarkably healthy but looked uncomfortably thin.

That summer my tiny savings and meagre allowance came to an abrupt end. As the summer holiday started I found myself with only the proverbial half-crown in my pocket, indeed in the world, and it was obvious that the drama school would have to be abandoned and a job of some sort found immediately. With some temerity I took myself to Wyndham's Theatre, where Gielgud was appearing in *The Maitlands*. I had never met him, was far from sure he would remember my name after the two or three weeks since the public show, but sent in my card. (In those days most drama students carried cheaply printed visiting cards, as a means of getting free tickets at some London theatres.) It was immediately after a mid-week matinée that I called and I was shown to his dressing room. Quite clearly he recognised me; and although he wasn't exactly welcoming – no doubt being used to calls from young aspiring actors – he was affable enough and very polite. I explained the necessity of obtaining work but didn't mention money. "They are holding auditions tomorrow morning," he said, "for understudies for a new play by Clemence Dane. With Gertie Lawrence. It's called *Moonlight is*

*Silver*. He gave me a rather sly amused look. "You might try for the understudy of Douglas Fairbanks Jr." (*That* was going to be no go for a start.) "Go there and say I sent you. And let me know tomorrow evening how you got on." Well, I went as instructed and was barely looked at – clearly I didn't fit the bill for understudying someone as tall, handsome and sophisticated as Doug Fairbanks. I reported back to John and he sent me to see Bronson Albery★ about a small part in *Queen of Scots*, which was being re-cast. Bronnie Albery was charming but my luck was out: casting had been completed a few hours earlier. The following day John advised me to go down to the Old Vic, where auditions were being held for bits and pieces in a forthcoming production of *Antony and Cleopatra*. I started my audition piece and after a couple of lines was greeted with howls of derision from the director in the darkened stalls. "You're no actor!" he shouted. "Get off the fucking stage!" (Some years later he was to direct me in Priestley's film *Last Holiday*.)

When I got back to Wyndham's that evening I had only fourpence left in the world and during the last two days had eaten two buns, two apples and had a couple of glasses of milk. John looked at me gravely when I told him of my Old Vic experience and then said, "I believe in you. But you are far too thin. You're not eating enough." On his make-up table was a pile of crisp pound notes. "Here's twenty pounds," he said, "until I can give you a job." He must have had the offer in mind and tried to hand me the money. Perhaps I was just too proud to accept, and rather light-headed from want of food, but twenty pounds was quite a sum in those days and I was terrified of getting into debt. Rather grandly, and certainly foolishly, I assured him I had no need of money. Leaving Wyndham's sad and worried, I started to wander back towards Westbourne Road but stopped on the way to gaze at the bills for a new play, called *Queer Cargo*, which was to open shortly at the Piccadilly Theatre. I decided that this might prove my last chance of a job and, on some strange impulse, instead of going to the stage door, took myself to the box office, where I happened to encounter the stage manager. Having talked to him for a few minutes he took me to a room, handed me a script and told me to read to him. The upshot was

★ Sir Bronson Albery (1881–1971), impresario and theatre-owner. The New Theatre, London, was renamed The Albery in his memory.

that I was given the understudying of nearly all the male parts (including Franklin Dyall) and told I would be walking on as a Chinese coolie, a French pirate and a British tar, all for the princely sum of three pounds a week. I was given one pound as an advance payment and treated myself to a steak, chips and a glass of beer round the corner.

Several weeks later I went to a matinée at the Old Vic and, seated in the pit, glimpsed Gielgud in the front stalls. In an interval I followed him to the coffee bar, not with the intention of speaking to him but just to be in his presence. He suddenly spotted me and came over, saying, "Where have you been? I've made enquiries for you all over London. I want you to play Osric in *Hamlet*. Rehearsals start on Monday week at the New Theatre." Through the kind offices of the stage manager at the Piccadilly I was released from my understudying and various disguises. My joy was almost out of control when I heard my salary in *Hamlet* would be seven pounds a week. But I hadn't foreseen the agony of rehearsals.

I revered Gielgud as an artist and was totally glamorised by his personality, but he was a strict disciplinarian, intolerant of any slovenliness of speech and exasperated by youthful tentativeness. He was a living monument of impatience. At that time he was thirty years old, at the height of his juvenile powers and, with *Richard of Bordeaux* behind him (I saw him in the part fifteen times), commanded a huge following throughout the country. He held his emperor-like head higher than high, rather thrown back, and carried himself, as he still does, with ram-rod straightness. He walked, or possibly tripped, with slightly bent knees to counteract a childhood tendency to flat-footedness. His arm movements were inclined to be jerky and his large bony hands a little stiff. A suggestion of fluidity in his gestures was imparted by his nearly always carrying a big white silk handkerchief. His resemblance to his distinguished old father was remarkable and he combined an air of patrician Polish breeding with Terry charm and modest theatricality. There was nothing he lacked, as far as I could see, except tact. His tactless remarks, over the decades, have joined the ranks of the happiest theatre legends of our time, and apart from their sheer funniness they have always been entirely forgivable because they sprang spontaneously from the heart without a glimmer of malice.

It was after a week of rehearsing *Hamlet* that he spoke "spontaneously" to me, with shattering effect. "What's happened to you?" he cried. "I thought you were rather good. You're terrible. Oh, go away! I don't want to see you again!"

I hung around at rehearsal until the end of the day and then approached him cautiously. "Excuse me, Mr Gielgud, but am I fired?" "No! Yes! No, of course not. But go away. Come back in a week. Get someone to teach you how to act. Try Martita Hunt; she'll be glad of the money." So I went back to Westbourne Road, sat on my narrow, rickety bed and had a litttle weep. I didn't dare tell Martita, who had become something of a friend, what had happened, as I felt she would be as upset as I was and might start telephoning John. I mooched around for a week, mostly walking in the London parks, and then, heart in mouth, reported back for rehearsals in St Martin's Lane. He seemed pleased to see me, heaped praise on my Osric and laughed delightedly at the personality (very waterfly) which I had assumed. I could swear I wasn't doing anything differently to what I had done before but suddenly, and briefly I was teacher's pet. "Motleys! Motleys, you should give him a hat with a lot of feathers, like the Duchess of Devonshire!"

We opened in November; the production was a sell-out, running for about ten months, and John's Hamlet was his definitive performance in the part. I watched most of it from the wings every single night, as did two or three others of the younger actors. At Christmas he gave me a handsome edition of Ellen Terry's letters in which he wrote, "To Alec, who grows apace," and then a quotation from Act Five, which has remained my motto throughout life, "The readiness is all."

I worked for him in *The Seagull, Noah* and *Romeo and Juliet* over a period of two years; left him for a season at the Old Vic under Guthrie's direction, and returned to him for the four plays he did under his own management at the Queen's Theatre in 1937: *Richard II, The School for Scandal, The Three Sisters* and *The Merchant of Venice*. He directed the Shakespeares, Guthrie* the Sheridan and Michel Saint-Denis the Chekhov. His companies were always happy and the only distress I experienced was just before we opened *Richard II*, in which I played the tiny but pleasing part of the Groom in the last act. We had a quick canter

---

* Sir Tyrone Guthrie (1900–71), director. Important influence in the theatre both in England and the USA.

through sections of the play on the morning of the first night and he said to me, "You're not nearly as good in the part as Leslie French was when I did it before. Try coming on from the right tonight, instead of the left, and see if that makes a difference." There was no time to rehearse it and very cheekily I asked, "Which right?" "Oh, have it your own way," he replied, wearily. "Do it as you've always done it. I can't be bothered."

In the theatre in our time there have been, and still are, some distinguished Johns and Jacks (to his family Gielgud was always Jack) but for over fifty years, if you said to a fellow actor, "I saw John the other day," there was never any doubt as to whom you were referring. In my opinion John Gielgud did more to liberate the English theatre from the fustian attitudes of the twenties and early thirties than any other man and paved the way for what is best in London today. He introduced new directors and designers from home and abroad, encouraged unknown actors and always cast around himself the finest established performers he could lay hands on. His humility as a man and as an actor is perhaps his most remarkable quality. And his enthusiasm for work leaves those of us ten years or so his junior flabbergasted and envious. But he is, of course, a workaholic and I doubt if he could even imagine a time when he would not be preparing a part; which is something for our constant delight and gratitude.

# JOHN
# MORTIMER

# JOHN MORTIMER

By profession a barrister, John Mortimer (b. 1923) is best known as the author of such plays as *Dock Brief* (1957) and *A Voyage Round My Father* (1970) and for the creation of the television series, *Rumpole of the Bailey*. In 1981, he adapted for television Evelyn Waugh's celebrated novel, *Brideshead Revisited*. One of the outstanding performances, as the hero's father, was given by John Gielgud.

# JOHN MORTIMER

Some things become a part of your whole life – and one of the best parts of mine is the voice of John Gielgud. It introduced me to classical acting and now I can't read *Hamlet* without hearing it, or see *Hamlet*, in these declining days of Shakespearean production, without missing it badly.

I suppose I must have been eleven when I first saw him at the New Theatre. The play was set in glowing autumn colours with an intelligent, ironical Prince whom John Gielgud has said he had great difficulty in remembering was not himself and who I, and I'm sure everyone else in the audience, clearly knew to be themselves. My father and I used to climb into dinner jackets and winged collars for these theatrical occasions, and always arrived ten minutes after the curtain rose, delayed by a prolonged dinner at the Trocadero. Although he was already a little hard of hearing my father had no difficulty with *Hamlet*: he knew the entire play by heart and could always say the lines, quite loudly, about three beats ahead of the actors.

My father's verse-speaking voice, from which I first learned Shakespeare, was, I suppose, derived from the actors he had first admired, Forbes-Robertson* and Martin-Harvey† and Frank Benson. If they, in their turn, learned their vocal style from the exaggerated intonations of Irving, verse speaking was more natural with the next generation of actors and reached, to my ear,

---

* Sir Johnston Forbes-Robertson (1853–1937) actor-manager.
† Sir John Martin-Harvey (1863–1944) actor-manager.

its highest peak with John Gielgud. So I was able to hear the old actors in my father's voice followed, almost immediately, by a more rapid, a more nervous and even more moving delivery from the stage. It was an extremely educative experience, and I had no inkling that at some distant date an actor might be born who would join the Royal Shakespeare Company and mutter, "To be or not to be", in a furtive and tuneless monotone, as though the greatest danger in any production were to allow the audience to recognise a familiar quotation.

Getting dangerously close to half a century later I dramatised Charles' father's part in *Brideshead Revisited* and, eternally and miraculously reliable, the Voice was still there to be used to equal effect in the most studied and perfected comic delivery. John Gielgud has always proved, if such an obvious proposition needs proof, that if you can play Shakespeare, you can play anything, and that there is no firmer basis for comic acting or writing than a thorough understanding of Shakespeare's great tragic heroes.

The welcome opportunity to write about the Voice is, perhaps, an occasion to remember the great performances of Shakespeare, and to feel sorry for those generations who, doubtless through no fault of their own, were unable to visit the New Theatre at the age of eleven. Although recent directors have done their best to conceal such an embarrassing fact, Shakespeare's plays are written in poetry. They rely on the power of rhythm, incantation and the distribution of hard and soft sounds, to heighten emotion in the same way that operas use music or religious services once used the beautiful language of the King James Bible to produce their various effects. My father was not musical, so he would repeat lines from Shakespeare rather as a man might hum a melody by Verdi or Mozart to keep his spirits up on a wet Monday morning in the Law Courts. In this way I know that "Nymph, in thy orisons/Be all my sins remember'd" was a beautiful line long before I had any idea of its meaning. Now if you know exactly what the line means, if you can feel its ironic point in the drama, your pleasure in the play is naturally complete, just as it is a pleasure to know what the Countess means when she sings *"Porgi amor"*. But to throw away all the music, all the pleasure in sound for the sake of a literal interpretation is a most self-defeating and sterile operation. A line of poetry doesn't only achieve its meaning from what it says, but also from the way that it sounds.

The great actors, of course, understood all that perfectly well. Olivier, with a different vocal instrument, uses notes as brilliantly and unexpectedly as any musician. John Gielgud, who loves and listens to a great deal of music and whom I have heard choose Mozart's Clarinet Concerto in radio programmes, knows just how to make sounds that are light, quick, comic and tender and quite suddenly and unexpectedly move you to tears. To my mind the falling standards in contemporary Shakespeare production began when directors began to speak contemptuously of Gielgud's "singing".

The decline in verse speaking has been accompanied by a decline in the teaching of poetry. Children no longer seem to learn poetry in school: when I was an early theatregoer we learned it (and verses once learned as a child remain with you for a lifetime) and heard it read by would-be actors who had settled for teaching but were yet profoundly affected by the John Gielgud delivery. Like all great original artists Gielgud's influence spread far beyond his own particular art. My father relied on the Gielgud *vox humana* in all his speeches in Probate actions, and I still hear echoes of it when I am making a final appeal to a jury. So what started in the great days of the Old Vic with a young, awkward actor whose one lugubrious line was, "Here is the number of the slaughtered French," can end up extremely usefully in a murder case down at the Old Bailey. However poor the imitation, the effect still appears to enthrall the jury.

I suppose, sitting at *Hamlet* all those years ago, I would have protested if anyone had told me that I was watching a great comic actor; but Shakespeare himself would have known better. You can't write tragedy without wit, irony and a sense of comic timing. *Hamlet*, to me, has far funnier lines than *Private Lives* and the heath scenes in *King Lear* provide better jokes than twenty years of television comedy. The one essential of comic acting is that it should be taken seriously, and John Gielgud correctly played John Worthing in *The Importance of Being Earnest* as a far more serious character than Hamlet and the result was, of course, hilarious.

Tony Richardson must have the credit for making Gielgud's comic acting available to the cinema audience when he cast him for a wonderfully dotty general in *The Charge of the Light Brigade*. It was through Tony Richardson that we met, so I have come to know John Gielgud a long time after I first heard him, and discovered the most entertaining of all actors, perpetually cheerful and looking delightfully and resolutely immortal. Prince Hamlet is now as I have described him elsewhere – "His back is straight, his head cocked, the nose like an eager beak clearing the air, the eyes hooded as if prepared to wince in fastidious disapproval at what the ever inquisitive nose might sniff. He has the bald head of a priest, the pink health of a retired admiral, the elegant suiting of what was once known as a 'man about town'." When I last enjoyed lunch with him he talked, as usual, incessantly, with hardly a pause for breath. His eyes turned to gaze about the room as though, through modesty, not wishing to take part in the conversation. His hands moved rhythmically and he said, "Tynan★ said I had only two gestures, the left hand up, the right hand up. What did he want me to do, bring out my prick?" The delivery of the line had not changed since I first heard him say, "Nymph, in thy orisons/Be all my sins remember'd!"

The last production I saw of *Hamlet* had a set which looked like the concrete end of a down-at-heel tower block in Deptford. Not only did the ruling house of Denmark look about as regal as a group of discontented sociology lecturers, they appeared to have no family relationship. The leading actor approached the lines at an uncomfortably fast trot and shied badly at any speech that was ever thought beautiful. Contrary to all indications in the text, Osric the water-fly was played as a bald Oddjob out of a James Bond movie and was present in every scene. At the interval I parted company with Elsinore and have never gone back.

My generation had the rare privilege of seeing Gielgud in the 1930s and Olivier and Richardson in the 1940s. I don't suppose Shakespeare has ever been done so well. I also have a head full of poetry spoken in that matchless voice. No one has a right to expect such presents. I would like to know where to take my eleven-year-old child to *hear Hamlet*.

★ Kenneth Tynan (1927–80), drama critic (the *Observer*, 1954–63); literary manager and later consultant, National Theatre (1963–73).

# PEGGY
# ASHCROFT

# PEGGY ASHCROFT

Peggy Ashcroft (b. 1907; created DBE, 1956) is among the half-dozen out-standing figures in the English theatre. Her range and versatility are astound-ing, having served playwrights as diverse as Shakespeare, Beckett, Rattigan, Pinter and Chekhov. She has been directed by Gielgud, or played opposite him in many notable productions, and they have been friends and colleagues for more than half-a-century. She is one of the people best qualified to judge his contribution to the theatre of our time.

# PEGGY ASHCROFT

In the last sixty years of English theatre there must be a myriad of memories and images of John Gielgud in the mind's eye of countless players and playgoers. To choose from such a wealth of recollections as I have might seem difficult, but in fact what lives most vividly for me are "early days" – the mid 1930s to 1940s – when I think John achieved not only a unique position but created a new situation in the theatre and one which was to determine the development of a very important part of the theatre.

It is fifty-one years since I first worked with John. In 1932 George Devine, then president of the OUDS, invited him to direct *Romeo and Juliet*, John's first production, with Edith Evans and myself as the Nurse and Juliet, it then being the custom of the OUDS to invite professional directors and professional actresses for their main productions. The rest of the cast were memorable: Christopher Hassall* as Romeo, William Devlin as Tybalt, Hugh Hunt† as the Friar, Terence Rattigan as First Musician, and George himself as Mercutio. John invited the Motleys – Sophie and Margaret Harris and Elizabeth Montgomery – to design the costumes. It was their first production, also.

The whole experience was exciting and unforgettable and it was a prologue to what was to happen to many of us under John's

---

* Christopher Hassall (1912–63), librettist (William Walton's *Troilus and Cressida*); sometime librettist for Ivor Novello and biographer of Rupert Brooke.

† Hugh Hunt (b. 1911), director. (Old Vic, 1949–53). Later an academic (Professor of Drama, University of Manchester, 1961–73).

inspiration and leadership in the late thirties. His energetic, fresh and dancing imagination was evident from the first rehearsal: his conception of the essential youthfulness of the play, which fitted his undergraduate cast, was something that inspired us all – amateur and professional; it had a marvellous zest and speed – an impulsiveness justifying the fiery quarrels of the Montagues and Capulets and the romantic follies of Romeo. And those qualities were something John was able to retain and develop in his definitive production at the New Theatre in 1935.

When he came to Oxford John had just concluded his successful season at the Vic – his first and historic *Hamlet* had been transferred for a season in the West End; he had followed this with Ronald Mackenzie's *Musical Chairs* and *Richard of Bordeaux* by Gordon Daviot. Then Bronson Albery invited him to do a season at the New Theatre virtually as actor-manager. It was there, from 1934–37, that he was to form the nearest thing to a permanent company in London since the pre-war era of Henry Irving and Beerbohm Tree. It is during that period, and the succeeding 1937–38 season at the Queen's Theatre, that I think John exerted one of the most important influences in our theatre that I can remember. Instead of just establishing himself as a great star, which he undoubtedly was, he was determined to put on productions of classics (not often to be seen in London at that time) and with as permanent a company as possible – a difficult task in those days of unsubsidised theatre. He had no problem in forming such a company. There was a growing feeling among many actors to be part of a company which could develop together, and in a sense supply the place of the national theatre companies of Europe. It was a wonderful opportunity for both experienced, seasoned actors and for younger aspiring ones.

John opened his new venture with a second production of *Hamlet,* followed by Obey's *Noah, Romeo and Juliet* and *The Seagull*; directing the Shakespeare plays himself and with Michel Saint-Denis and Komisarjevsky doing the Obey and the Chekhov respectively. He has always had the highest regard for great directors: he knew then the value of learning and working with such men as Granville-Barker, Saint-Denis and Komisarjevsky, as he was later to value Peter Brook and Peter Hall.★

The Motleys continued as an integral part of John's company.

★ Sir Peter Hall (b. 1930), director of the Shakespeare Memorial, later Royal Shakespeare Theatre, 1960–73; director of the National Theatre since 1973.

Their contribution was a major one. They had a studio and workshop opposite the New Theatre, and where all our sets and costumes were made. It was not only their working place, but it became, as it were, the actors' club. There we could spend our hours off from rehearsal – and largely through this we became the close-knit company that we were. We had no permanent contracts during that first New Theatre season, but we nearly all stayed together, or rather were kept together, when John eventually decided to do a further season at the Queen's Theatre in 1937–38 with four productions: *Richard II, The School for Scandal, Three Sisters* and *The Merchant of Venice*. John's Richard had already been acclaimed at the Vic, his Joseph Surface was one of the most dazzling comedy performances I can remember, his Shylock was challenging and unusual – a fairy-tale monster, defying sympathy. *Three Sisters* was the particular triumph of the season, Saint-Denis demanding seven weeks' rehearsal (then unheard of!), and I think the company, under his influence, reached its climax as a wonderfully welded ensemble. John's dream was realised.

They were halcyon days in which was created almost a family of actors: Edith Evans, Gwen Ffrangcon-Davies, Barbara Dillon, Marjorie Fielding, George Devine, Glen Byam Shaw, Alec Guinness, Harry Andrews, George Howe, Frederick Lloyd, Leon Quartermaine, Laurence Olivier (only, alas, with us for Romeo) and Stephen Haggard for Constantine, augmented at the Queen's by Anthony Quayle, Richard Ainley, Michael Redgrave, Angela Baddeley, Rachel Kempson and Carol Goodner. John was a natural leader, an inspiring – if provoking – director, constantly changing his mind due to his abundance of ideas, but his authority we never questioned even if we were given plenty of scope for argument. It was out of this "stable" that many future events and movements grew. In 1939 a new season was planned for the Globe Theatre, starting with *The Importance of Being Earnest* and *The Cherry Orchard* – the latter in rehearsal, and the former being played when war was declared and the season brought to an abrupt end.

Of course the war changed everything – gradually the younger men were joining up and what we had been building seemed to be lost though I think most of us felt we would rebuild at a future date. John played in two very fine productions at the Old Vic – *Lear* and *The Tempest* – directed by Granville Barker and

George Devine. This was John's second Lear and Barker's production was to influence him in two later productions at Stratford. In 1944–45 he embarked on a further season of his own at the Haymarket: *Love for Love*, *The Circle*, *Hamlet*, *Midsummer Night's Dream* and *The Duchess of Malfi*. It was a brave effort but inevitably it was a more sober company and a depleted one: Michael, Alec, George, Glen were all in the forces; older actors joined us, such as Leslie Banks, Cecil Trouncer, Max Adrian. Yvonne Arnaud sparkled brilliantly in the first two productions and Marion Spencer and Rosalie Crutchley joined the ensemble. We survived the buzz bombs and the V2s; we saw the end of the war and looked to the future.

There was a definite style, I think, in all these productions, John's strength lying in his devotion to the clarity of the text, his visual taste and discrimination in their presentation and his insistence that the entire cast should be at the highest possible level. Why – after that final Haymarket season did John never venture into the same managerial field again (except as the moving spirit in the 1952–53 season at the Lyric Hammersmith with Paul Scofield and Pamela Brown)? Perhaps his involvement as an actor or director, very often both, in the service of other organisations: the Memorial Theatre, Stratford, when he did his magnificent production of *Much Ado About Nothing*, his perform-ances as Angelo, Cassius, Leontes, and two further Lears and Prosperos as well as numerous foreign tours and West End productions were as much as he wanted, or could manage, to do – many riches. But out of those first years at the New and the Queen's he developed a group of actors who met and re-met with him and with each other, and who have been part of the National Theatre development under Laurence Olivier and Peter Hall, and part of the RSC under Hall and Trevor Nunn. All this showing, I think, the vital continuity that has been such a great factor and a strength in our post-war theatre. It manifested itself in yet another way when George Devine started the English Stage Company at the Royal Court – a very different theatre, dedi-cated to finding new writers and beginning a new and revolu-tionary era in theatre attitudes; but he still drew on past experi-ences and on actors who had worked together and could be re-deployed, joining forces with younger, newer talents. Years later, after George's death, John was to play for the first time at the Royal Court, giving one of his finest performances in David

Storey's *Home*, which was a new step for John in the world of modern playwrights, and in company with his oldest friend and partner of earlier days, Ralph Richardson. How much George would have enjoyed that.

To the younger generation today, although he is a legend, he is known largely for his brilliant cameo appearances in film and television, one towering major performance in the film *Providence* and two stunning stage roles in *Home* and Harold Pinter's *No Man's Land*. His charm and charisma have never flagged – and who knows what he may have up his sleeve for us yet? Perhaps his ability to keep his friends – even if not at a particularly intimate level – has been one of the secret strengths of his career; that, and his total honesty as well as generosity to all his fellow actors. To be a friend of his and a colleague – for a lifetime – is something that I cannot prize too highly. To his public – nationally and internationally – well, there is only one John Gielgud.

# HAROLD
# HOBSON

# HAROLD HOBSON

Harold Hobson (b. 1904) succeeded James Agate as drama critic for the *Sunday Times*, a post he held from 1947–76, the years that marked the greatest change in the contemporary theatre. He was made CBE in 1971; his knighthood followed in 1977, and was the first to be awarded for service to dramatic criticism.

# HAROLD HOBSON

I once said to John Gielgud that he had given himself to the theatre as, in the Middle Ages, men and women gave themselves to monasteries and nunneries, and with something perhaps of the same reason. Monks and nuns were frequently people who had heard the voice of God summoning them to a life of remote piety. But often, too, the monastery or nunnery was a refuge for younger sons and girls with no dowry for marriage; for people, that is, whose family had failed to provide a life for them.

There is no doubt why Gielgud entered the theatre, and, the world forgetting, by the world forgot only for short periods, made in it for himself an illustrious career, one of the most illustrious, in fact, in the entire history of British drama. He was devoted to it from childhood. In it he found life and emotional satisfaction and intellectual stimulus. Yet I cannot help feeling that there was a subsidiary feeling which impelled him, albeit perhaps unconsciously, to the stage. He talks about the theatre a great deal. So does Donald Sinden. But there is this difference between them. Sinden is absorbed by every detail of theatrical history. He reveres the great figures of the past as if they were saints of his personal religion. I believe that he never goes upon the stage without carrying with him some relic, maybe a glove or a handkerchief, previously worn by one of his great predecessors.

Sir John's theatrical talk, as those will know well enough who have listened to him on radio or television, is not about Edmund Kean or Sarah Siddons. It is all about his bubbling joy in recalling

Ellen and Kate and Fred, every one of them a Terry, every one of them a member of his own family. I have the impression that this glittering and mercurial man of the world, this dazzling conversational star of the Garrick,★ who has brought the art of the impishly desired involuntary *gaffe* to its highest peak of perfection, is in reality a family man without a family except among the dead; and, perverse, brash, impertinent and reckless though it be to say so, that it would have eased many problems in his career, and supplemented many personal characteristics, if he had had a family of his own, and been surrounded by a wife and children.

He certainly has one gift that comes in very useful to a married man: I mean, a capacity for enduring affection. He first knew Richard Goolden (the celebrated and beloved Mole of *Toad of Toad Hall*) when they appeared together at the old Oxford Playhouse in the early 1920s. When I went up to Oxford in 1924 I saw them both in Shaw's *Candida*, Gielgud as a lithe and even athletic Marchbanks (he sprang from the centre of the stage to perch on the arm of Candida's chair without flinching) and Goolden, a meek but mischievous curate. I am not aware of their having played often together after their later triumph in *The Cherry Orchard* (Goolden was dropped from his part of Firs when the play transferred to London) but the memory of their old association never seemed to fade in Gielgud's mind. When Richard died nearly sixty years later he took immense pains to come up from his country home to Chelsea Old Church to read the Lesson. I need hardly say that he did it magnificently. The incomparable words – "O death, where is thy sting? O grave, thy victory?" – rolled through the aisles of the church with a sweet and triumphant majesty. As I sat waiting to give the address, exalted by the nobility of Gielgud's voice, I marvelled at the conviction and asserted but unassertive power that could be put into these sublime, improbable words by a man who had once told me that he had not an atom of religion in his composition (but in this he exaggerated).

Marriage is a frightening thing. "To marry," said Stevenson, "is to domesticate the Recording Angel. Once you are married, there is nothing left for you, not even suicide, but to be good." (That is putting it a bit strong; and many married men have judged differently. Nevertheless there is something in it.)

★ The Garrick Club in London. A club to which actors, writers, lawyers, publishers and politicians, among others, belong.

Stevenson goes on, "Times are changed with him who marries: there are no more by-path meadows, where you may innocently linger, but the road lies long and straight and dusty to the grave." These indeed are alarming words; and Gielgud may well all his life have been intimidated by such considerations. (He did in fact tell me so, thirty years after our first acquaintance in Oxford, when I sat between him and Alan Napier★ in Germer's saloon in King Edward VII Street, all three of us waiting to have our hair cut.)

Marriage is also said (though by a lesser authority on the subject than Stevenson) to slow a man down. "Down to Gehenna or up to the Throne, He travels the fastest who travels alone." What is more certain is that marriage steadies a man. Gielgud's career has certainly been erratic; it could well have done with that bit of steadying and of common sense which a wife may bring. It has reached tremendous heights more than once, and also fallen to some sickening depths. A touch of regularity would have saved a lot of unhappiness. There are some zigzags even less attractive than Stevenson's long and straight and dusty road to the same goal. Gielgud was recognised as a rising young actor even at the Playhouse, when he was only twenty; he was a famous Lear at the Old Vic when he was twenty-five, and achieved the greatest popular triumph of his life before he was thirty, in Gordon Daviot's *Richard of Bordeaux*. It is amazing, it is heart-lifting, that having achieved fame so early in his youth he should still have it, undiminished, when he is old. But there have been some difficult hurdles in between.

After *Richard of Bordeaux* the successes still went on. He discovered a very good young new playwright, Ronald Mackenzie, who was unfortunately killed in a car crash. In 1937 and 1938 Gielgud directed a season at the Queen's with a company which included Peggy Ashcroft and Michael Redgrave (it was Redgrave's Bolingbroke in *Richard II* that first suggested that one day Gielgud might be supplanted as our leading Shakespearean actor). Both public and critics immediately perceived that this season was one of the high points of achievement of the British theatre. It received enormous and judicious praise. Curiously enough, Gielgud at the time did not perceive the magnitude of what he had done, though he came to realise it clearly enough later. There were too many quarrels in the company, he said to

★ Alan Napier (b. 1903), actor.

me. Agate called him "Our First Player". Yet I don't think that Gielgud admires Agate quite so much as one would expect. After all, it was Agate who made the fortune of *The Cherry Orchard* by calling it the best play in London. "But he wanted to be my Egeria," said Gielgud, "and hated me when I wouldn't let him." It was after that, though not because of it, that the troubles began. Had Gielgud had a wife to assure him of the excellence of the Queen's season whilst it was still on, still more to convince him of it, he would have acquired a self-confidence he soon came to need.

It was when Olivier and Richardson returned from the wars and had marvellously successful seasons at the old New Theatre in the middle and late 1940s that Gielgud began to be subjected to unbearable strain. When Richardson and Olivier were knighted and he was passed over, in 1947, he gradually realised that the leadership of the stage was sliding away from him. He felt no jealousy; one of his finest traits is that jealousy is entirely un-known to him. But at this time one felt that he was beginning to know a new sadness. He is particularly conscious of the passage of time, and though he was still comparatively young he told me that he was always aware of "Time's wingèd chariot hurrying near." The sensational rise of Olivier and Richardson was some-thing that he could neither ignore nor forget. Yet he was never uncharitable; he did not argue with himself – as Olivier did when Richardson was honoured before him – that he had done work which merited recognition just as much as theirs. One day in the Ivy restaurant he mused in a sort of way at Olivier's exceptional grandeur. "Larry lives *en prince*," he murmured, almost to himself. There was some surprise in his voice, even possibly a doubt whether such magnificence could last. But there was no envy or resentment.

He was delighted, when his own honour finally came in 1953, that it was in the Coronation Honours list. "That gives it a special kind of quality, don't you think?" he said to me, again at luncheon, but this time at the Caprice. It seemed that he was back with all his old authority, but then he suffered the advent of the *avant garde* with Samuel Beckett's *Waiting for Godot* in 1955. This brought in a style of drama with which Gielgud was totally out of sympathy. The position he had regained with his knighthood was eroded, and though he played many important plays, both at Stratford and in London, his stature diminished in comparison with that of Olivier. So much so, that some time later, Olivier himself became genuinely concerned. The *Evening Standard*, as it then was, inaugurated a series of annual awards, which gained great prestige, and one day I received a message that Olivier wanted to see me. A superb Rolls arrived at my home, and carried me in splendour to the great man. Olivier was much agitated. He had the year before received the coveted *Standard* award for Best Actor, and he had heard that it was likely that he would get it the second time. "This is distressing," he said. "Getting an award means nothing to me. It makes no difference at all to my reputation. But if I get it again, it will be another slap in the face for Johnnie. It is a cruelty that mustn't be allowed to happen. I want you to resign from the selection committee." I admired his sympathy for Gielgud, and I admire it now. But what that had to do with my resigning from the committee (of which I was not an important or influential member) I have never been able to understand. But I saw that Olivier meant well, and so I resigned. The award was duly offered to Olivier, and, somewhat to my surprise, he accepted it.

One of the most dramatic moments in *Richard of Bordeaux* came when Richard's wife, Anne of Bohemia, asked him what he would do if his enemies defeated him. He bid her not to be afraid, "for if the heavens fell, I know that you would still be there." When the heavens did fall, Gielgud, as I have shown, had many friends, but he had no Anne of Bohemia, no comforting home, no abiding domestic love to sustain him. That I cannot help regarding as a thing to be pitied. But the friendship he has received from others he has returned in full measure. He remembered Richard Goolden, and he remembers Gwen Ffrangcon-Davies, who played Anne of Bohemia half a century ago. He loses no opportunity of making known his conviction that this actress should be created a Dame of the British Empire.

I never admired Gielgud more than I did in those days of tragedy, out of which in recent years he has happily come once again into the full sunlight of success, not only regaining his position on the stage, but making new reputations for himself on the screen and in television. He showed that he could impose grace, style, and distinction even when directing a play as pretentious, irritating, and absurd as Enid Bagnold's *The Chalk Garden* (1956), which ran for hundreds of nights at the Haymarket. A year later he created a remarkable Prospero at Stratford. Here was no kind old man, ready to forgive everyone in a universal benediction, even though he had been shamefully abused by his usurping brother. In fact he hardly appeared old at all. He was lean, clean-shaven, and grizzled, just as Caesar had been at the height of his victories. He certainly looked noble, but his look was harsh and dangerous. From revenge for his lost dukedom, and hatred for his evil brother, Gielgud's Prospero was a man who, to win all power, had looked into the pit and been defiled.

It was not however the quality of Gielgud's performances, high as this was, that roused my admiration, so much as the courage and determination with which he had won his way back into the hearts of the public by putting himself upon the stage alone, without scenery, and without the support of other players. He did this with the recital that the famous and sympathetic George Rylands★ had compiled from Shakespeare under the title of *The Ages of Man*. Soon after Prospero, Gielgud appeared in this recital in New York. But before that, in 1957, he had given it at the Edinburgh Festival, and later I saw him in it at the Haymarket and in Dublin.

It was a remarkable performance which began rather tentatively, and the unusual heat of the afternoon at first made the audience somnolent. For the first quarter of an hour we were conscious only of a tall and graceful figure, beautifully and unostentatiously dressed, reading noble verse in an equally noble voice. It was admirable; it was civilised, but it was, given the accompaniment of a heat to which Edinburgh is rarely accustomed, a little soporific. Then Sir John sprang back from his reading desk, broke his reliance on his text, and shocked our drowsiness into intent awareness with an extremely vigorous rendering of the Queen Mab speech. Yet I don't think that this was done in his best manner. He was beyond question enthusiastic about Queen Mab. She had clearly made a deep impression on him. But, as I wrote in the *Sunday Times* at the time, his enthusiasm had a suggestion about it of an advertising agent recommending a line of goods in which he happened personally to believe. But the speech, if it had not the high distinction which comes so easily to Gielgud, was alive, and for the first time it set the audience cheering.

★ George "Dadie" Rylands (b. 1902), Fellow of King's College, Cambridge; influential English academic. Directed Gielgud's 1945 Hamlet.

Thereafter success followed success. In Hotspur's sarcastic attack on the fashionable young man who would have gone to war had it not been for the horrid guns; in Troilus' "Single, famished kiss, Distasted with the salt of broken tears" which Gielgud spoke with a sad, withdrawn affection, as if the actor were at one and the same time feeling the pain of parting, and yet placing it, from the viewpoint of an immense distance, in the right perspective among a host of other sorrows; above all, in the musical despair of *Richard II*, in his luxurious savouring of the perverse pleasures of humiliation and defeat; it was in these things and many more that we had the big outbursts, the harmonious whispers, the awe and majesty of an excited intellect, of a superb presence, of an incomparable voice.

This Edinburgh Festival of 1957 had a great effect in changing my view of Gielgud. Hitherto I had regarded his greatest effects as those in which he portrayed men whose nerves were strained almost to the point of breakdown. For me his most memorable moments had been in *Richard of Bordeaux* when, in a frenzy of youthful anger and passion, he clutched his great cloak round him as he was attacked on all sides by rebellious uncles. That, and his scornful reply at the end of the second act, when he was asked in what did he put his trust for the defence of his rights and his divinity, he answered in a voice like a silver trumpet "In twenty thousand men-at-arms, paid regularly every Friday." My throat gulped at these words; waves of triumph swept through me. But I did not, then, nor for long afterwards, fully appreciate the mellifluous beauty of his voice, nor its delicate mastery of rhythm. It was in *The Ages of Man* that I first came to my senses. I am particularly glad that it was in Edinburgh that this remarkable entry into sanity on my part was effected. For I consider Edinburgh as the grandest, the most perfect of cities in its union of the classical and the romantic, and many are the things that I owe to its festivals.

I was impressed even more with what Gielgud had accomplished on the road back to fame and unquestioning acceptance. On my next visit to Paris I was struck by the great gift which Gielgud had given to the reputation of the British theatre in France. During the 1950s, whenever I visited Paris, I was besieged by questions from eminent figures in the French theatre as to the standing in Britain of various of our celebrated players.

Olivier, Richardson, Redgrave, Peggy Ashcroft and Vivien Leigh had all been seen in Paris by the leading French actors and actresses. I am sorry to say that they had all been disappointed. Olivier they respected, but their admiration of him was muted. And as for Vivien Leigh, they marvelled that such a waxwork (exquisite though waxworks may sometimes be) could seriously be regarded as an actress at all.

What prevented the French from making a full response to Olivier was, I think, his way of speaking verse, which personally I find very exciting. But it is quite different from Sir John's. This was shown in the recital itself, when he came to the "sear, the yellow leaf" speech. Two years before, at Stratford, in one of his greatest performances, Olivier's voice, when he reached the phrase "troops of friends", suddenly soared, as if in incredulous astonishment that in the course of mortal existence a man should be the cause of friendship. Olivier gave us in those lines a poignant realisation of what it means to have lived a long life, and to have inspired no love in any human creature.

The effect of this on me had been tremendous, the leap in Olivier's voice from the humdrum to the ecstatically elegiac, revelatory. But I do not think that the French are very fond of these abrupt changes of tone, these changings of the pace of the music. They think themselves the masters of verse speaking, as in the long tradition of Racine and Corneille and certain plays of Molière, they are. It is not, I realised, and said at the time, Gielgud's way to subsume the pity and loveliness of an entire speech in a single, carefully chosen phrase. He sees the speech whole, ordered and regular in its music and architecture, and he presents it to us, not as Olivier does, luminous in one revealing detail, but in all its unbroken beauty.

It was not until the French critics who had come to the Festival, along with Madeleine Renaud and Jean-Louis Barrault,* returned to Paris and made their reports that France learned that Britain had an actor who could speak verse as well as they could, and in their manner. Barrault and Madeleine were especially generous in their tributes to what they had heard.

Gielgud is generally considered to be nervous of new experiments in the theatre. He feels safe when encompassed by the verse of Shakespeare, "If you forget it, you can make it up as you

* Madeleine Renaud (b. 1903) and her husband Jean-Louis Barrault (b. 1910), distinguished French actors who founded a company of international renown.

One of the earliest photographs.

*Above:* The White Butterfly in *The Insect Play*, 1923. *Left:* Trofimov in *The Cherry Orchard*, 1925.

Richard of Bordeaux, 1933-34.

Hamlet, 1934

Hamlet, 1944.

*Above:* Romeo, with Peggy Ashcroft as Juliet, 1935. *Left:* Richard II, 1929. Costume design by Motley.

*Above:* First major film role in
*The Secret Agent* with Peter Lorre,
Madeleine Carroll and Robert
Young, 1935. Directed by Alfred
Hitchcock. *Right:* Noah, 1935.

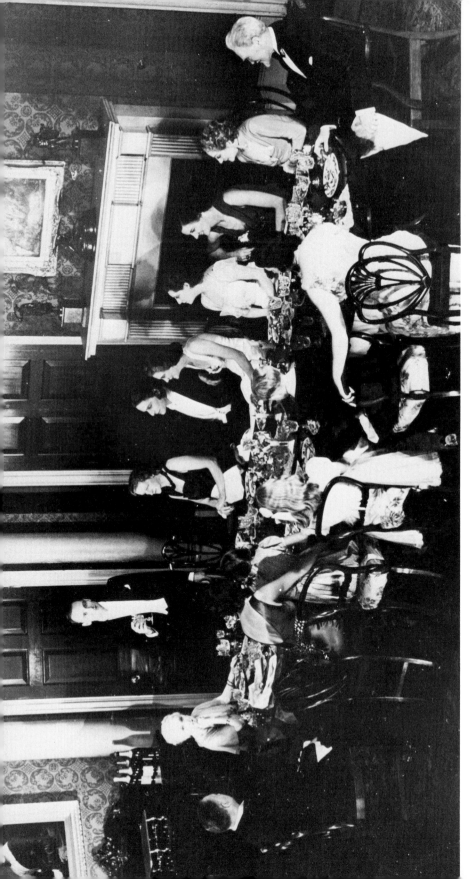

Making the Grand Toast in *Dear Octopus*, with Marie Tempest at the head of the table, 1938.

go along," he once remarked in the Garrick, but the inconsecutiveness of contemporary drama disconcerts him. He was invited to play in Beckett's *End Game*, but refused. He says he can't understand it, or endure it. "When I saw it I had practically to be chained to my seat." He walked out of *One-Way Pendulum*, but was thrilled by *Look Back in Anger* and *The Caretaker*. He admits that *Waiting for Godot* has some good writing in it, but he thinks it sordid and pessimistic. He is inordinately sensitive to blasphemy. He saw Jean Genet's *The Blacks* in New York, and says that he didn't know where to look. Deeply shocked, he left the play during the interval without understanding what it was all about. By Gielgud's judgment the things that get Genet into such a frenzy (and are the source of such fine prose) are fetishes of a special kind. He hangs the portraits of murderers and pimps on the wall of his room, and prays to them. That, says Gielgud, is horrible. When I interviewed him on this he was amazed that I did not have the same emotion of disgust. With Genet, he went on, the performance makes you nervous. You can never be sure that something indecent isn't going to happen and in a mixed audience this is embarrassing. He cannot understand why highbrows are always so delighted with the improper and the randy. Gielgud agrees with the man who said, "I don't care what they do so long as they don't do it in the streets and frighten the horses." This hypersensitiveness is highly complementary to Gielgud's fastidiousness, but it seems to me to suggest a certain instability, an unsureness, very likely to attack a man who has passed his life in loneliness outside the rough and tumble of domestic existence, without even the solace of sport. He never plays cards, or cricket, or golf. He can't ride, or even drive a car (though perhaps he has learnt to do that in later years). He has nothing but the theatre.

In all the sixty years that I have known Gielgud I have never seen him otherwise than poised and happy, buoyed up by irrepressible enthusiasm. Nor is this a façade. It is the real Gielgud. And yet I have always felt that there is something in him which life has not satisfied, and for which he is constantly searching. Of all the people I have known in the theatre, he is the man who goes about most constantly questioning. He gives me the impression of someone who deep down in himself knows that there are fundamental things which he does not comprehend, and who is determined to find them out. To realise that there are vast spaces of life and art of which one has not the secret, and to go on searching so long as life lasts to find out their meaning is perhaps the highest form of wisdom. This wisdom Gielgud has: despite the apparent confidence with which he faces the world, no man is better aware of the existence of the well of the unknowing.

It is odd, for example, that he is so profoundly shocked by the blasphemy of Genet. If he believes in no religion himself, as he told me he does not, why should he be outraged that someone should indecently attack it? As I said to him, religious people themselves are not particularly upset by blasphemy. "That," he replied, "is because it does not shake their faith." In fact at one time he himself passed through a religious phase. This was during the last term at Westminster, just before I saw him on the stage for the first time. In his final schooldays he was constantly dashing off to the Brompton Oratory. He supposes now that what attracted him was the incense and the ritual. His feeling was theatrical, not truly religious. In any case he had an acute disillusionment when he came to be confirmed. At his confirmation he expected a great light to shine upon him. It did not shine, and the failure of the illumination to appear is something that has affected him ever since, and left in his life a void he has not apparently been able to fill. Yet religion still stirs him with wonder. He marvels that its force is so powerful that men have been willing to suffer martyrdom for it, and that it has inspired them to build masterpieces such as Chartres Cathedral. It is curious that he does not (or did not) mention the Authorised Version of the Bible, which moves me more profoundly than either Chartres or even Amiens. It is curious, I say, because, as at the memorial service to Richard Goolden, with which I began, and on other occasions, I have heard him read from it with splendour, apparent conviction, and superb pride.

But then, he can, he asserts, act anything which he can understand, even if he does not believe in it. In Graham Greene's *The Potting Shed* (1958) he played the part of a man who, without knowing it, had been raised from the dead. I found Gielgud's performance of the resurrected boy masterly, though I was aware that personally he did not believe in the resurrection of this boy, or of Christ, or of anyone else. If ever, I felt, there could be presented on the stage a good man from whom God has removed his presence, then in this play Sir John presented him. In dark, flannel trousers, James Callifer, till his moment of salvation, with cheekbones sharp under shaven flesh, looked like a man carrying within him a world of Polar ice. The poignancy of the perform-ance lay in Gielgud's capacity to suggest that it is ice which, even at its thickest, yearns for the sun.

So in a way, or such is my impression through the long years I have known him, does Gielgud. I will not say that Greene was able to bring to Gielgud the illumination which his confirmation had strikingly failed to provide. But he was able to explain every question that Gielgud asked about the resurrected boy. He avoided no enquiry, however searching. There had been a time when Gielgud had wanted to play *The Family Reunion*, and he tackled Eliot in the same way that he had tackled Greene. But not with the same results. Eliot would explain nothing. So he was unable to play *The Family Reunion* because its author could not, or would not, make him understand it. Gielgud found the same thing with Fry. He felt that both Fry and Eliot wished their work to be surrounded with a penumbra of mystery which only the elect could penetrate. Greene, on the other hand, would explain everything. This is why Gielgud, though an unbeliever, could in some cases play expositions of belief. There are two things in the theatre which exalt me. They are faith, which Gielgud can arouse, and love. They are both things which I would wish to possess abundantly.

I remember on one occasion asking him if he had ever thought of marriage, for it is a fundamental basis of this essay that he is essentially a family man, though he has no family. He said no, because he could not bear taking the responsibility for someone else's life, or of children. He had never thought of marriage. It seems to arouse in him the fastidiousness which is inspired in him by Genet. It brings him to quite extraordinary convolutions of enquiry and logic. Thus when he was asked to play Othello in 1961 he was much preoccupied by the question whether Desde-mona was still a virgin when she arrived in Cyprus. He wrote to George Rylands about the problem, for it is a feature of Gielgud's career that he has always had a deep respect for academics. Rylands said that Shakespeare did not much bother about that sort of thing. But Gielgud still felt it essential to know, and he found two lines of text (he did not tell me which they were) that suggested that Desdemona still actually *was* a virgin. Otherwise, he said, he could not have played the part. This seemed tremendously important to him, for if Othello had not rushed to consummate his marriage before leaving Venice, Gielgud believed that it proved that Othello was something more than the impulsive animal he is often supposed to be.

But though Gielgud may be too afraid of responsibility to attempt marriage, he is avid of it in the theatre. There are some actors, such as Paul Scofield, who are content just to play their parts. But Gielgud is not like that. He interferes with everything, and this has occasionally led to fearful quarrels and made him enemies. But this does not last. There are not many people in the theatre whom he hates, he says: not more than half a dozen. Few theatrical tasks daunt him. There was a memorable example of this when he took over from the sad John Burrell the job of directing *The Heiress* only five days before the play was due to open at the Haymarket. Burrell had been part of the triumvirate which had ruled the Old Vic in the triumphant days of Olivier and Richardson, but he was making a disastrous hash of *The Heiress*, and was sacked. This hurt Richardson, who had a very tender heart, to the quick. Gielgud was summoned. He rushed to the theatre the day that Burrell was dismissed, and was greeted by Sir Ralph with the distressing words, "This morning we have been present at a man's assassination." Nothing daunted, Gielgud set himself to the entire remodelling of the piece, and less than a week later it opened to enormous success.

Yet even in the theatre Gielgud's confidence sometimes wavers, and, as I say, he has no one at home to sustain him in hours of doubt. He will take up a play with unbounded enthusiasm, and then begin to wonder. He has not the tremendous self-confidence of an Olivier, but seeks guidance and advice. He found help chiefly in Granville-Barker. He describes a rehearsal with him like being at a masseur's. You felt bruised and broken, but with muscles functioning you never even suspected of being there. Komisarjevsky also helped him. He combined a sense of music, of colour and movement, and of the distribution of sound and silence which later he found only in Peter Brook. Peter Brook, he says cunningly, is a director who gets on very well with actors he gets on well with.

Faith. Well, I have written of faith. But love? This is a more delicate task. The lines about his wife being with him even if the heavens fell (in *Richard of Bordeaux*) are very moving. They are the king's words and they should catch the heart. The tears should come into one's eyes. I remember saying to a girl I knew,

"But no tears came." She told me that she herself had wept bucketsful. Perhaps I was only trying to impress her, and sound cynical and worldly. Who knows? Anyway, it is a long, long time ago.

I have always found it touching that when Gielgud, after being introduced into the modern drama by Alan Bennett in *Forty Years On*, really came into his own in the contemporary theatre, it was in a play by David Storey which bore the ironical title *Home*. And it is in a contemporary play, Julian Mitchell's *Half Life*, that Gielgud made me shed the tears which were dry in me in *Richard of Bordeaux*. At the very end, when Gielgud as the old scholar, after learning that the youth he had loved half a lifetime before had been a sham and a liar (or so I remember) stumbled out of the garden through the door into his house with a stifled sob, I felt the emotion I had not found in *Richard of Bordeaux*. Here indeed was love, though not the love that leads to marriage. Gielgud is a great actor, and is today at the summit of his achievements, his talent ripened, not diminished by age.

# IRENE
# WORTH

# IRENE WORTH

Irene Worth was born in Nebraska, USA, in 1916, but only two years after her American debut in 1942 came to London to study with Elsie Fogerty. A leading actress on both sides of the Atlantic, she has played opposite Gielgud often and is a close friend. She was awarded an honorary CBE in 1975.

# IRENE WORTH

"Lead me!" Those were the last words of the play, and John spoke them with a tone of such gravity and beauty that I can still hear the resonance of his voice. I was on stage with him, as Jocasta, impaled on a golden spike. We were in a production of *Oedipus* for the National Theatre when it was in its last days at the Old Vic.

Peter Brook had put together one of the most profound productions of our generation. David Turner had chosen to translate Seneca's *Oedipus*, and Ted Hughes "realised" it for us during our rehearsals and extemporisations, shifting the text, embellishing it with his powerful crags of words. John, in a simple movement, put two small black patches on his eyes and that was his blindness. His long staff struck the golden stage each time his right foot moved him towards his exit. But how had this economy come about? John followed Peter's vision.

I think John dislikes experimental theatre more than anyone I know and yet he has been in two unforgettable revolutionary productions which ran totally counter to the romantic tradition he stands for.

How did he come to be in the startling Noguchi *Lear* which George Devine directed? The answer must lie somewhere in his genes and in his spirit which makes his love for the theatre so faithful that nothing can faze it. He must act, he must work, he must grow, he must be part of it; he is like a restless thoroughbred. I think he feels almost a sense of sin if he's not working. His discipline is fierce. He does not need to rest, he does not want a holiday. He eats sparingly and falls asleep whenever he wishes. He is always on time. He is loyal and he is modest. It is the theatre which comes first with him, not his own ego and not a need to show off. He husbands his bright gifts.

When I first began to act I read an interview in which he said, "Acting is half shame, half glory. Shame at exhibiting yourself, glory when you can forget yourself."

This then was the raw material for a man of stature and humility. We arrived for the first rehearsal of *Oedipus*. John was immaculately dressed, as always, but at the end of that day it was quite obvious we were in for a long haul. From the next day on John appeared in corduroy trousers suitable for crawling on the floor. For that was our first discipline the next day: we were all lined up behind a kind of starter's line and told to crawl carefully, with shut eyes, to the other side of the room. If we touched *anyone* in this blind, worm-like scramble, we would contract the plague.

Does this sound foolish? It is not foolish to the actor; to the actor becoming the person; to the person who lives in fear, in Thebes.

These exercises continued to grow in complexity. The aim was to create, contain and then release the most frightful emotions which man can build in tragedy. It is an exhausting process and more painful than going to the dentist. We are trained as people to contain but not to release these emotions. John is too elegant even to dream of self-indulgence and his nature rebels at the thought of crying out in anguish.

"The highest and lowest of God's creatures understand tragedy, the others find it merely unpleasant." I paraphrase John's great friend Isak Dinesen,★ but it was to this huge discipline that he now committed himself: to find the tragic sound.

I don't know how it happened that I got caught in the rehearsal room when Peter took John to one side and began to urge him towards the sound needed. Not an external cry, but the cry which no one can hear, only feel.

The company had gone home, they two were alone on one side of the room, I on the other. Peter's voice was low. I tried to

★ Isak Dinesen (1885–1962). The pseudonym of Karen Blixen, Danish author of *Out of Africa* and *Seven Gothic Tales*.

become deaf. It got later and later, darker and darker. No lights. If the atmosphere had been altered by a ripple the concentration would have been disturbed and the exercise ended. John worked with Peter on and on, trying to get it right. I, trying not to breathe, very slowly tore the lace off a huge old prop cushion, in silence, like the boy who was given sheets to tear against his pain.

It was over at last and we three limped home. That was my friend and colleague who had wrestled with the angel, but who was wrestling with whom I do not know. His great good nature and his respect and faith in Peter gave him monumental courage. The same was true of his devotion to Granville-Barker. This is the simplicity which has made his character and which makes people love him as a hero. And from this passion came the incredible "Seems, Madam?" – a peerless Hamlet which I saw in 1945. Conscience on a rapier's point. Anger, not bad temper.

The gestures of tradition are within him and he will not depart from this breeding. His courtesy has its special grace. This extends to crew and company alike. The flowers are sent, the notes arrive, the best and funniest letters are posted from wherever he is in his travels. Sometimes his shyness trips him up. The gaffes! He doesn't always say what he means. The jokes abound. The ubiquitous *Times* crossword. The puns. He is Shakespeare's brother in his love of puns.

At the dress rehearsal of *Oedipus* we were on the set for the first time. It was all gold . . . the floor and the sides, and in the centre was a huge golden box which revolved very slowly, sending off glancing flashes of light. The riddle contained within it would unfold, the sides come down, first one, then two, as each scene progressed until all the sides were down, the box gone, the riddle read, the sacrifices made, the city cleansed.

Peter was in the empty stalls and called out "Irene, try your spike before we begin the last scene." Ronald Pickup had just finished his cataclysmic final speech as the Messenger and was standing with John in the wings. I was to expire on this golden spike in a metaphor which involved horrendous gymnastics, more arduous, it seemed to me, than anything demanded even of dancers.

"How is it?" called Peter.

"A bit short," I called back.

"Sorry," said Peter.

The merriment was now reaching epic proportions.

"What can we do about that?"

"Well," I pondered, "perhaps we need a plinth!"

"Plinth Philip or Plinth Charles?" came from John in the wings, doubled up with laughter. The entire theatre was rocking, the strain was over, the energy recharged, the fun of hard work renewed. I suppose people who word hard value essentials.

He leads a company as no other and brings his own radiance. Blake wrote, "He whose face gives no light shall never become a star." John's light shines in the firmament and I say with gratitude, "Lead me."

# PETER
# BROOK

# PETER BROOK

When he first worked with Gielgud in 1950, Peter Brook, then aged twenty-five, was generally regarded as the *enfant terrible* of the English theatre. Since then he has become one of the major forces in the theatre throughout the world. He was made CBE in 1965. Three years later, he directed Gielgud in Senecca's *Oedipus*, a production recalled by Irene Worth, and also remembered by the director.

# PETER BROOK

We had assembled for the first reading of *Measure for Measure* at Stratford. It must have been about 1950. I had never worked with John Gielgud before, nor had most of the actors. The occasion was nerve-wracking, not only because this time the reading was going to take place in the presence of a legend. Gielgud's reputation at the time inspired both love and awe and as a result each actor was thrilled to be there and dreading the moment when he would have to be seen and heard.

To break the ice I made a short speech, then asked the actor playing the Duke to begin. He opened his text, waited for a moment, then boldly declaimed the first line. "Escalus!"

"My lord?" came the answer, and in those two words, hardly audible, one could hear the panic of an actor, wishing for the ground to open and playing safe with a token murmur.

"Peter!" From John came an impulsive, agonised cry of alarm. "He's not really going to say it like that, is he?"

The words had flown out of John's mouth before he could stop them. But just as swiftly he sensed the dismay of his poor fellow actor and immediately was contrite and confused. "Oh, I'm so sorry, dear boy, do forgive me. I know, it'll be splendid. Sorry everyone, let's go on."

In John, tongue and mind work so closely together that it is sufficient for him to think of something for it to be said. Everything in him is moving all the time, at lightning speed – a stream of consciousness flows from him without pause; his flickering, darting tongue reflects everything around and inside him: his wit, his joy, his anxiety, his sadness, his appreciation of the tiniest detail of life and work, in fact, every observation once made is spoken; his tongue is the sensitive instrument that captures the most delicate shades of feeling in his acting and just as readily produces gaffes, indiscretions and outrageous puns which are just as much part of the very special complex called John.

John is a mass of contradictions which happily have never been resolved and which are the motors of his art. There is in him an actor-reactor, quick on the draw, answering before the question is put, highly strung, confusing and ever so impatient. Yet tempering his John-in-perpetual-motion is the John-of-intuitions, who winces at every excess, his own or others.

It is always thrilling to work with the impatient John. Directing him is a dialogue, a collaboration – it has to be, it could not be anything else. You begin to suggest something, "John, perhaps you could enter from the right and . . ." Before you can finish your sentence, he has applauded the idea, agreed, is ready to try it, but before he has taken two steps he has seen five objections, ten new possibilities and is proposing, "But, what if I come from the left . . ." and if that in turn suggests something new to you, he will already have discarded his thoughts to explore your own.

He loves "changing the moves" in rehearsals and of course he is right. "Moves" in the theatre are just the outer expression of ideas and, one hopes, ideas change and develop all the time. But many actors have difficulty keeping up with his tempo, become resentful, long to be told once and for all what they have to do and then be left alone. For such actors, John sometimes seems maddening, impossible. It is said that as he leaves the stage after a last performance he is still changing the moves.

He seems to have no method, which is in itself a method that has always worked wonders. His inconsistency is the truest of consistencies. He is like an aircraft circling before it can land. He has a standard, intuitively perceived, whose betrayal causes him deep pain. He will change and change indefinitely, in search of rightness – and nothing is ever right. For this reason, it has always been absolutely necessary for him to work with the best actors and his generosity towards them in performance comes from his need for quality which has always been infinitely more important to him than his own personal success. When he directs, often he neglects his own performance and one has

g Lear. *Right:* Stratford, 1950.
*w:* in the production designed
samu Noguchi, 1955.

*Above:* John Worthing in *The Importance of Being Earnest* with Gwen Ffrangcon-Davies, 1939. *Left:* Duke Ferdinand in *The Duchess of Malfi* with Marian Spencer, 1944.

*Above:* Thomas Mendip in *The Lady's Not for Burning* with Pamela Brown and Richard Burton, 1949.
*Right:* Benedick in *Much Ado About Nothing,* 1950.

Leontes in *The Winter's Tale,* 1951. In the dressing room . . .

. . . on stage.

*Right:* Julian Anson in *Day By the Sea* with Ralph Richardson and Irene Worth, 1953. *Below Right: The Ages of Man,* first performed in 1957.

*Left:* Angelo in *Measure for Measure,* 1950. *Below:* Cassius (third from right) in the film *Julius Caesar* with James Mason as Brutus and Marlon Brando as Mark Antony, 1953.

*Above:* Prospero, 1940. *Left:* Prospero
1974.

grown accustomed to seeing him in a leading role standing to the side, back turned to the audience, an observer, deeply involved in the work of others.

Despite his great gifts as a director, as an actor, he needs to be directed. When he develops a part, he has too many ideas: they pile in so fast, hour after hour, day after day, that in the end the variation on top of variation, the detail added to details all overload and clog his original impulses. When we worked together, I found that the most important time was just before the first performance, when I had to help him ruthlessly to scrap ninety per cent of his over-rich material and remind him of what he had himself discovered at the start. Deeply self-critical, he would always cut and discard without regret. When we did *Measure for Measure* he was inspired by the name of Angelo and spent long, secret hours with the wigmaker, preparing an angelic wig of shoulder-length blond locks. At the dress rehearsal no one was allowed to see him, until he came on to the stage, delighted at his new disguise. To his surprise, we all howled our disapproval. "Ah!" he sighed, "Goodbye, my youth!" There were no regrets and the next day he made a triumph, appearing for the first time with a bald head.

The last time we worked together was Seneca's *Oedipus* at the Old Vic. I accepted to do the play uniquely for the pleasure of working with John again after many years, although in the meantime my own way of approaching theatre had greatly changed. Instead of starting with a first reading, I now spent a long period doing exercises, largely involving bodily movement. In the company, there were a number of young actors, very eager to work in this way and there were also several older actors for whom all these methods seemed dangerous new fads. The young actors angrily despised the older actors in return and, to my horror, they regarded John as a symbol of a theatre they had rejected.

On the first day, I suggested some exercises that demanded considerable physical involvement. We sat in a circle and the actors tried the exercise one by one. When John's turn came, there was a moment of tension. What would he do? The older actors hoped he would refuse.

John knew that after the confident young actors he could only appear ridiculous. But as always, his reaction was immediate. He plunged in. He tried, he tried humbly, clumsily, with all he could bring. He was no longer the star, a superior being. He was quite simply there, struggling with his body, as the others would be later with their words, with an intensity and a sincerity that were his own. In a matter of seconds, his relation with the group was transformed. It was no longer the name nor the reputation of Gielgud that mattered. Everyone present had glimpsed the real John; he had bridged the generation gap and from that moment he was held in true admiration and respect.

John is always in the present; he is modern in his restless quest for truth and new meaning. He is also traditional, for his passionate sense of quality comes from his understanding of the past. He links two ages. He is unique.

# MICHAEL
# BILLINGTON

## MICHAEL BILLINGTON

Born in 1939, Michael Billington has been drama critic of the *Guardian* since 1971, and has seen Gielgud act since the mid-1950s. He is able to assess the actor in the heat of theatrical and social change which has taken place in the last twenty-five years.

# MICHAEL BILLINGTON

I first saw John Gielgud on stage at Stratford-upon-Avon in the winter of 1955. I was, at the time, a theatre-mad Midlands schoolboy deeply enthralled by the saturnine grandeur of Laurence Olivier who that summer at Stratford had inscribed his Macbeth and Titus Andronicus forever on my memory. I am not sure what I expected of Gielgud (then heading a second Stratford company that had been touring Europe and the provinces with *Much Ado About Nothing* and *King Lear*) beyond style, presence and a famously beautiful voice. Whatever I expected, I was certainly in for a shock.

The Gielgud *Much Ado* was already famous: a piece of glorious Renaissance high comedy that had first been seen at Stratford in 1949. But the *King Lear*, directed by George Devine and designed by an American-Japanese sculptor, Isamu Noguchi, was extraordinary. The prevailing style was Oriental. Gielgud himself played Lear with his oval face framed by what looked like a mane of white horsehair. His costume, as Lear descended further into the pit of madness, got full of progressively larger holes until there was almost nothing left. Even his throne was a triangular gold affair that, at the time, someone rudely compared to a metaphysical lavatory seat. I had come expecting to see the High Priest of English acting: what I saw was an exciting performance by an actor obviously wide open to experiment.

This to me is a vital point. Olivier is often seen as a trail-blazing radical, Gielgud as a stylish conservative. But my early experiences of Gielgud were of an actor ready to take hair-raising risks.

Indeed the next time I saw him he was playing Prospero at Stratford in Peter Brook's 1957 production of *The Tempest*. Instead of the expected Ancient of Days, what one got was a grizzled, angry, sun-bronzed, semi-naked figure in a hempen cloth who had clearly been nursing his grievances as carefully as his daughter Miranda. Instead of an oratorio (which the play can all too easily be), one got real drama with Gielgud making it touch-and-go whether charity would win out. Over a quarter of a century later, I can still recall his cry of "Though with their high wrongs I am struck to the quick" which struck a mounting arc of fury. In the end benison and sweetness triumphed; but Gielgud made it a hard-won victory, lending the role an emotional dynamic I have rarely seen since.

Gielgud, in short, surprised me; and he has gone on surprising me ever since. His reputation is for music, sublimity, a slightly etherealised passion: in fact, his performances are much more rooted in observable truth than that suggests. He also has a gift for comedy that over the years has become fine-tuned. I first spotted it, apart from his Benedick, in his Gaev in the Michel Saint-Denis *Cherry Orchard* at the Aldwych early in 1962. This is one of those strange theatrical productions that, if ever you mention it to any of the actors involved, seems to cause an involuntary shudder ("You mean you *liked* it?" they cry with incredulity). My memory is of Chekhov played with a down-right emotion I had been taught to associate with the Moscow Art Theatre; and of Gielgud drifting through life, scarf casually draped over one shoulder and silver-topped cane in hand, in a state of perpetual moonstruck fantasy like some pre-revolutionary Billy Liar. His apostrophe to the bookcase had a daffy, sentimental excess; he swanned through rooms taking imaginary pot-shots with imaginary cues; and when he cried "I shall become a financier" (on being offered some second-rate job in a bank) it established Gaev as a character cocooned in self-delusion. This was superb comic acting: the creation of a privileged, elderly child living in a perpetual Chekhovian state of might-have-been.

Over the years I have never yielded up my initial perception of Gielgud as an actor ready to tread the path of adventure (my hunch is that he is very trusting of directors) and very skilled at ironic comedy. One has, of course, seen him woefully miscast as in a notorious Stratford *Othello* where he looked, in Tynan's words, like a "coffee-stained Leontes" and where lines like "rude am I in my speech", fell implausibly from his lips. And I was never quite persuaded by him as the eponymous hero in a National Theatre version of *Julius Caesar*. He phrased the part with impeccable intelligence ("The cause is in my will – I *will* not come," he announced, refusing to go to the Capitol); but he struck me as a singularly beneficent ruler rather than an over-weening tyrant and the result was to make the conspiracy look like a gratuitous attempt to kill off the best verse speaker on the English stage.

But my view of Gielgud as a questing, comic character-actor of genius has been supported by a lot of hard evidence. I remember him still as Orgon in a much under-rated Guthrie production of *Tartuffe* at the Old Vic: Gielgud played Orgon definitively as a gullible, noble goose, smiling seraphically at Robert Stephens' bumpkin-hypocrite, muttering "Poor fellow" and peering myopically at Tartuffe's palms for signs of stigmata when the arch-deceiver knelt before him in a Christ-like posture. I retain a clear image of him in Charles Wood's *Veterans* sitting astride a prop-horse in a kepi surrounded by the synthetic smoke of cinematic battle and listening patiently while Bob Hoskins' sparks invited him to pop in for a cup of tea back home whenever he was passing. And, of course, there was his famous Spooner in Pinter's *No Man's Land*: demob-suited, sandal-shoed, the epitome of all pub-poets and lending a precise, rueful comedy to lines like "My mother remains, I have to say, a terribly attractive woman in many ways. Her buns are the best." This was Gielgud at his perihelion: delving into his tenacious memory and making a character manifest before our eyes.

There is, however, one performance of Sir John's that I haven't mentioned and that illustrates many of my observations about him as an actor: his appetite for risks, his gift for comedy, his under-rated ability to characterise. That performance is *The Ages of Man* which I have seen several times and in many places: in London at the Queen's, at the Royal Shakespeare Theatre in Stratford, at the newly opened Nottingham Playhouse. It can, rather clinically, be described as a solo Shakespeare recital. But it is more, much more, than those rather cold words suggest. It offers a guide, in George Rylands' nippy editing, to Shakespeare's own breadth and humanity. It reveals Gielgud's quicksilver ability to move from, say, the stoic serenity of the fifth-act Hamlet to the racked agony of the tormented Lear. But I believe it does something else of great importance: it nails the myth that Gielgud is simply a superb musical instrument, an ambulatory violoncello, a producer of great sound. Obviously, there is profound aesthetic pleasure in listening to his voice. But, like all great actors, he uses his voice to give language a concrete, witty, specific meaning and not simply to lull us into ecstasy. He doesn't simply speak verse: he *acts* it. And he demolishes, at a stroke, the supposed division between the music-makers of yesterday and the hard realists of today.

Listen (which thankfully one can still do on record) to his conflation of the great speeches of capitulation and surrender in *Richard II*. Here, if ever, is a chance for the pure organ-stop approach. And yet Gielgud minutely characterises the verse, running the full gamut of anger, irony, contempt, tear-stained self-pity and downright mockery. He has a matchless feeling for the architecture of a speech, taking a series of lines on a single breath and building to a thrilling crescendo. But, within that, there is rare sensitivity to the weight and sense of each particular phrase.

Take the seventeen lines beginning "What must the king do now? must he submit?" At first Gielgud is all humble surrender. But when he comes to "must he lose the name of king?" he surrounds those lines with an aura of majesty as if the mere memory of monarchy stirred great thoughts in him. How does he do it? Partly by treating "king" almost as if it were a two-syllabled word – or at least one that could be stretched out to infinity. But, having dwelt lovingly on the remembrance of divine authority, he pauses for thought and then cries very simply "O' God's name, let it go." He then comes to a famous passage of structured rhetoric ("I'll give my jewels for a set of beads") but, instead of luxuriating in it, gives each phrase equal measure until he comes to the climactic thought, "And my large kingdom for a little grave." Here he shows Richard captivated and excited by the conceit of an obscure, humble burial place with the voice rising in a quiver of expectation. He plays with the thought, dallies with it and he slides into self-laceration as he imagines being buried "where subjects' *feet* may hourly trample on their sovereign's head." The final hard consonant in "feet" is knocked home like a nail, giving you the smell, the texture, the sound of common feet parading above his mortal remains. And then comes the final lapse into self-pity as Richard imagines himself, after death, being literally downtrodden.

All great acting is a form of practical criticism: it takes the words and looks afresh at what they are saying. And Gielgud in the *Richard II* speeches cuts away the fussiness and dead-wood of his earlier versions (also preserved on record) and gets direct to the bone. He gives us Richard's malevolent irony on "Here, cousin, *seize* the crown"; the sense of a huge physical burden being shed on "I give this heavy weight from off my head"; and, astonishingly, the very sensation of splintering glass on the mirror-hurling line, "As brittle as the glory *is the face*", with a slight caesura before the last three words and then an intemperate, vein-bursting, manically destructive cry. That is not disembodied word-music. That is great acting.

*Richard II* may be the showpiece. But throughout *The Ages of Man* Gielgud characterises the language giving us sense as well as sound. His Mercutio is virile, hectic, fanciful, filled with adrenalin-buzz; and Gielgud subtly delineates the effect Queen Mab has on different characters. He suddenly slows the tempo, thickens and deepens his voice for the nose-tickled parson ("Then dreams he of another benefice"); he speeds up again for the soldier and when he talks of "drums in his ear" actually produces the rattling, vibrating timbre of a beaten drum. And when he comes to Hotspur he again makes a clear demarcation between the impetuous, fiery, intemperate Northerner and the effete, perfumed lord who comes demanding Hotspur's prisoners in King Henry's name. The cornerstone of the speech becomes "For he made me mad" with the voice hitting an angry, rising curve and justifying Hotspur's choleric abandon.

The more one considers Gielgud as a verse speaker, the more one begins to realise that the distinctions often made between himself and Olivier are too crude and facile. The common assumption is that Olivier is an impressionist, colouring and highlighting a single phrase in a speech and often throwing away the rest; Gielgud, on the other hand, is seen as a consummate musician with a unique feeling for the symphonic movement of a speech. Olivier, Tynan once said, gives you a single reading of a line: Gielgud several readings at once. But this strikes me as so much taradiddle. Obviously, there are vast differences in temperament between the two actors. But both have the ability to carry a Shakespearean thought through on a single, sustained breath (what else is it that makes Olivier's "Once more unto the breach" so exciting); and both have the knack of picking out the key phrase that lies at the core of the speech. In "To be or not to be" Gielgud hinges everything on the way the dread of something after death "puzzles the will", pausing both before and after those three little words to give a sense of a bewildered, divided, tormented humanity.

Critics have, in fact, helped to build up the myth of Gielgud as an artful melodist whose verse-speaking traditions have been shattered by the new realists. How often has one read that some raw, jagged, violent new Hamlet has finally got away from the Gielgud tradition simply because he fractures and splinters the verse. But I see nothing unrealistic about Gielgud's method. What he shows is the infinite pliability of the iambic pentameter and how, within a respect for the basic Shakespearean metre, one can achieve all manner of effects. Gielgud's verse speaking is fantastically *supple*, totally unsentimental.

If you doubt that, concentrate simply on his rendering of the final speeches of *King Lear*. Here is no abstract music but a man at the end of his life veering between powerful, contradictory emotions like a ship rocking in a storm. On "Howl, howl, howl, howl," Gielgud builds to a peak of plangent anguish. But with "This feather stirs: she lives" hope quickens and the voice achieves a giddy delirium at the prospect of Cordelia's resurrection. "And my poor fool is hang'd" takes Lear back to the abyss with the voice echoing resonantly like a coin flung down on marble. But at the last there is a quiver of possibility, a laugh even, on "Look on her, look – her lips –" at the imagined stirring of life; and this Lear dies in a fever of ecstasy crying "Look there, look there." Never shall I forget Gielgud on stage in *The Ages of Man*, Savile Row-suited and impeccably elegant, taking us to the extremity of emotion with nothing but Shakespeare's language and his own iron-clad technique to help him.

I have dwelt on Sir John's realism and characterisation because I think there is a danger he may go down to posterity as the embodiment of a formal, patrician style of acting: nothing, in my book, could be further from the truth. I have said little about the man himself, partly because my few encounters with him have largely been in the context of newspaper or radio interviews. But I have always been struck by the fact that one goes expecting to meet a grand personage and comes away having met a witty, acute, communicative man, pleasantly eager to have a theatrical gossip. As everyone knows, he can be very funny; and I well remember turning up in Split for the location-shooting of a forgotten Napoleonic movie called *Eagle in a Cage*. The movie involved Gielgud and everyone else in a number of tiring, perilous ascents of a particularly craggy rock-face. But, of course, it was Sir John who instantly dubbed the film *Climb and Punishment*.

When we last met, it was in a Broadcasting House studio to record an item celebrating Sir Ralph Richardson's eightieth birthday. Sir John was characteristically perceptive about his old friend, highlighting a quality of anger in his acting that few people had seized upon. After the recording he told me that he had just come from a memorial service for Marie Rambert. He recalled that only recently he had attended a similar service for Kenneth More. "Sometimes," he said with mock-weariness, "I feel as if I may as well stay on for my own." But his poker-backed bearing, the vitality of his conversation, his fascination with the latest novels, films and plays belied that entirely. As we parted in Portland Place, I was forcibly struck by the way Sir John brought to life itself the very qualities I had noticed when I first saw him on the stage nearly thirty years ago: the sensation of a bright mind ever young and a ravenous appetite for the new.

# ALAN
# BENNETT

# ALAN BENNETT

Alan Bennett (b. 1934) was one of the four young men (the others were Peter Cook, Dudley Moore and Jonathan Miller) who captivated London and New York in the revue, *Beyond The Fringe* in the early 1960s. Without entirely abandoning his career as a performer, Bennett has become a leading dramatist both in the theatre and on television. His first play was *Forty Years On* (1968) and in it Gielgud made his entrance as the Headmaster into what J. C. Trewin calls 'the newest theatre'. The events surrounding the production were recorded by the author in a diary, parts of which have previously been published in the *Observer*.

# ALAN BENNETT

*Forty Years On* was my first play. It is set in Albion House, a rundown public school on the South Downs, where the headmaster is about to retire. To mark the occasion, staff and boys devise an entertainment, "Speak for England, Arthur", which is set during the Second World War and looks back over the period 1900–1940. I had put the play together in 1967 and sent it to the National Theatre. It came back pretty promptly with a note from Ken Tynan, saying that it wasn't their cup of tea but might have commercial possibilities. With a cast of nearly thirty it seemed unlikely. I showed it next to Frith Banbury, who suggested to Toby Rowland, a director of Stoll Theatres, that they should present it. I wrote a second draft and the play eventually went into pre-production in March 1968. The director was to be Patrick Garland, the designer Julia Trevelyan Oman, and with what seemed to me at that time great presumption Toby Rowland sent the script to Sir John Gielgud. Would he like to play the Headmaster?

These are some extracts from my diary of the months that followed.

MAY 24TH, 1968
Patrick and I have supper at Toby Rowland's house in Smith Street to meet Gielgud. He is taller, squarer than he seems on stage. I am very nervous, knowing that if it comes to "selling" the play I won't be able to say much. Not to worry, as Gielgud talks all the time, telling story after story, head back on the sofa,

famous nose in profile. He recalls a tour of India during the war, remembers Oxford, unspoiled in the 1920s as Waugh describes it in *Brideshead*, and the OUDS production of *Richard II* he directed at the Playhouse with Florence Kahn, Beerbohm's wife, playing the Duchess of Gloucester, while Max sat shrinking with embarrassment in the stalls.

He is currently appearing at the National in Peter Brook's production of *Oedipus*, which I don't let on having seen. Stories are rife of the indignities to which the actors have been subjected; some, representing plague-stricken Thebans being tethered to pillars in the auditorium, where latecomers regularly take them for programme sellers. The cast are dressed in matching sweaters and slacks in a tasteful shade of tan and look like a Bulgarian table tennis team. Gielgud is very loyal to Brook over all this, saying simply that while it has been hard going he is sure the difficulty and embarrassment of it have done him good.

I am beginning to be conscious that nothing is being said about the play when suddenly, disconcertingly, Gielgud starts straight in on what is wrong with it. His first target is the twenty-five boys we have decided would be the minimum requirement for the school. He would prefer none at all: they will fidget, they will distract, surely cardboard cut-outs would be better? He is not put out when one opposes such suggestions, but he does not abandon them easily. (A few months later, when the play is happily running in the West End this suggestion of cardboard boys will seem a huge joke, but this evening it seems to augur a very rough ride.)

At eleven we break off to watch a trailer for Patrick's television programme on Dr Johnson. The sound doesn't work and the aerial is faulty. We sit gazing at this grey, silent pantomime, with Gielgud getting steadily more bored and irritated. Patrick is seemingly unaware of this and we are stuck there, until luckily the set breaks down altogether and we get back to the play.

A quarter of an hour before he leaves Gielgud announces that he does not intend to commit himself until the final draft of the script is finished and at 12.30 he strides off into Chelsea as fresh as when he arrived.

"Don't be shy," he says as he shakes hands. "It is very funny." I take this to mean he has decided against it.

The headmaster in *Forty Years On*, 1968.

*Left:* Lord Raglan in *The Charge of the Light Brigade,* 1967. *Below:* Sir Geoffrey Kendle in *Veterans* with John Mills, 1972. *Right:* Oedipus, 1968.

Harry in *Home,* 1970 . . .

. . . Spooner in *No Man's Land,* 1975, with Ralph Richardson.

Charles Ryder's father in *Brideshead Revisited*, 1981.

Major movie star. *Arthur,* 1980.

John Gielgud, 1983.

JUNE 20TH

A second meeting with Gielgud, lunch at The Ivy. He is now reconciled to the boys but having seen John Lennon's *In His Own Write* at the National, he is worried about the back projections. More stories. Of Emerald Cunard, who summoned him to dine at the Dorchester during the Blitz. "And a very dull meal it was, chicken and ice cream. Emerald surveyed the table and rang for the butler. 'And where is the butter?' 'There is no butter, ma'am.' 'No butter? But what is the Merchant Navy doing?' " He returns to the play. "I am not sure about singing 'Forty Years On'. After all, it was Churchill's favourite song. And he is dead. And everyone knows that. I think it's terribly dangerous."

"Oh no, it isn't."

"Isn't it? No, I suppose not."

And off he goes again on his ever-rolling stream of anecdote.

Many of the figures featured in the play he has met . . . Nijinsky, Diaghilev, T. E. Lawrence, Ottoline Morrell. There is a parody of a lantern lecture on Lawrence which I had earmarked for myself. Gielgud makes no bones about wanting to do it. I point out primly that it wouldn't fit in with the character of the Headmaster to deliver it. He pooh poohs this. I'm in no position to disagree and besides he will do it far better than I could, but I'm thankful, as I see a large chunk of my part disappear, that I'm the author of the piece not simply an actor in it.

Once this is settled he gives his final approval to the script and we get down to casting.

JULY 9TH. HER MAJESTY'S

Yesterday and today spent auditioning boys at Her Majesty's on the set of *Fiddler on the Roof.* As an audition piece we ask them to read a passage from Leonard Woolf's autobiography, *Beginning Again.* "Who am I supposed to be, then?" asks one kid with golliwog hair and velveteen pants. "Leonard Woolf?" "I was in George Bernard Shaw," says another. "I played the drums."

Many belong to a species of stage boy only distantly related to childhood by their small size. All the other attributes of boyhood, youth, gaiety, innocence have long since gone. Squat creatures, seemingly weaned on Woodbines, these are the boys who have been in *Oliver!* Lionel Bart has cut a swathe through the nation's youth like the 1914–18 war. They are the new Lost Generation.

In the afternoon, when we have been going for about an hour, there is a quavering voice from the darkness of the Upper Circle. "Could you tell me when you're going to start, please?" It is an old lady, who has come for the matinée of *Fiddler on the Roof* on the wrong day.

AUGUST 26TH. STOLL THEATRES
A reading of the play this evening in Prince Littler's boardroom. It had been set for the previous Friday, but the management felt that Gielgud would be so upset by the bad reviews of *Don Giovanni*, his production at the Coliseum, that they had put it off. In fact he is quite perky. "Bloody but unbowed," he murmurs, "bloody but unbowed." I meet three of the players . . . Dorothy Reynolds, Nora Nicholson and Robert Swann for the first time.

Patrick is nervous and makes a fatuous opening. "We're just going to read the play and I think the best thing for us to do would be to . . . read it . . . starting at the beginning."

Gielgud starts in on his opening speech at a furious speed, occasionally breaking off to say, "That's wrong, isn't it? You can cut that. That's too long." We come to the end of the play. Gielgud reads the last speech superbly and there is a long silence. It is broken by the Stoll company manager, Rupert Marsh. "You'll have to do it quicker than that. We can't be late closing the bar."

In the subsequent discussion Gielgud sits silent and detached while everyone talks round him. He doesn't like the beginning of the play within the play. It is a parody of Oscar Wilde set in 1900.

"They weren't playing Wilde in 1900," he says. "They didn't revive *The Importance* until 1911." I don't think this matters. "But the audience won't understand. It's too sudden. Couldn't you do something about the Wilde case? I remember my mother saying she wasn't allowed to read the papers during the trial." This doesn't seem to me to be particularly useful and I don't want to get involved in all the tiresome Wilde business. But in the end Gielgud proves to be right and not until Wilde's name is actually introduced before the parody does it really take off.

SEPTEMBER 2ND. DRURY LANE
Bank Holiday Monday and the first rehearsal on stage at Drury Lane in the shadow of Sean Kenny's enormous *Four Musketeers* set. The principals rehearse upstairs and the boys below stage in

120

the Ballet Room. Paul Eddington, who plays the Housemaster, is a man after my own heart, brooking no interference with physical comfort: he is greatly put out that due to the holiday there is no coffee. Eventually tea is procured in the cracked cups belonging to the stage hands. Gielgud doesn't want it, nor Nora Nicholson, the old nanny in the play. They don't like interruptions.

In the morning the plotting goes ahead slowly, with Gielgud sitting apart doing his eternal crossword. I have heard stories that he is apt to fill in any old word that is the right length. I sneak a look and am disappointed to find this a myth. He learns his script by writing it out in a neat hand on the page opposite the text. "I am a very bad study. After fifty, one gets much worse."

He is full of ideas for his own part and for the play, many of them good, some cock-eyed. The cock-eyed ones take a lot of getting rid of. He is quite frank about this, saying that when he directs he always warns the actors he will come up with a dozen ideas, only one of which will be of any help. At the close of the afternoon he wants to scrap the whole of the ceremonial opening we have spent hours blocking, in which the boys enter singing round him. Why not make it just a quiet chat on stage?

"I think I should speak to the audience," he had said at the first reading. "I am very good at that. I like singling people out."

"I can't bear speaking to the audience," he says this afternoon. "And it's so old hat, singling people out. I can't bear that." (The job of persuading him to address the audience will turn out to be the biggest problem Patrick has to face. But when, in the nick of time, Gielgud is persuaded and begins to do so it transforms the whole production.)

Patrick and I go down to the Ballet Room to listen to the singing. Carl Davis, who has arranged the music and is to play the organ on stage, has already got the boys looking and sounding like a group. A lot of them smoke furiously, as if afraid of being caught. The singing sounds well, solid and moving and better in this echoing room than it will sound on stage.

In the evening I go through the cuts, taking out a parody of Dorothy L. Sayers' *Man Born to be King*, lest it should be thought simply a revue sketch, which it is. We lose some good jokes.

SEPTEMBER 6TH. HER MAJESTY'S
The papers are full of a fat contract landed by Millicent Martin.
During a lull in rehearsal I come across John G. at the back of the
stage, dancing round by himself, singing "Who cares about
Millicent Martin? Oh, who cares about Millicent Martin?"

SEPTEMBER 14TH. HER MAJESTY'S
Nora Nicholson, who is nearing eighty, refers to death in a most
unmorbid way. "I will do it," she says, when offered a film part,
"if I am still here. I've just moved into a flat with a three and a half
year lease. That should just about see me out." She first appeared
with John G. when he acted a butterfly in *The Insect Play*, and was
herself in Benson's company. When she auditioned for Benson
he enquired what parts she had played; she couldn't think of any
and went home disconcerted, only to remember that she'd
played Juliet. She is the nanny in the play, and had a nanny
herself, who, when anyone laid an uninvited hand on her arm,
would say, "Don't touch me there, something might form."
Today the management takes us out to lunch at Rules. Speculat-
ing on what might be under a monster dish cover, Nora says "I
hope it's not boiled baby. Still, I'd rather have boiled baby than
boiled mouse." As I leave her in the King's Road, she shouts after
me, "And remember to buy me a very big wreath."

SEPTEMBER 23RD. DONMAR STUDIOS
A good day today, the first on the set which has been put up in the
Donmar Studios, near Seven Dials, so that we have a week in
London to get used to it before we open in Manchester. It is on
several levels, which up to now have been represented by
different coloured tape on the stage floor. The boys adapt
themselves splendidly to the new three-dimensional reality and
play with a new zest and spontaneity which pulls the play
together. John G. and the older principals are nervous of the
number of stairs.

SEPTEMBER 25TH. DONMAR STUDIOS
Gielgud telephones at 9.30 to say he has flu. We rehearse without
him. It is a bloody day. The boys are restless and thunder about
the set, drowning the dialogue and irritating the principals.
George Fenton, the biggest and gentlest of the boys, is sick. He
lies down on the child's bed we use in the Nanny scene and as we

go off to lunch he is fast asleep with a gollywog cradled in his arms. It is the one nice thing about the day. We have a bad run-through in the afternoon in which I several times lose my temper and nearly clout some of the kids. It is getting too like school. One realises how important John G.'s presence is: he is always impeccably polite and any slight flurry of temper is followed by an instant apology. His modesty and good behaviour infect everyone else.

SEPTEMBER 26TH. DRESS REHEARSAL
Prince Littler comes in the afternoon to see a run-through, the last before the dress rehearsal in Manchester, where we open. He is the chairman of Stoll, who own all the theatres on Shaftesbury Avenue. "I see we've got the bricks and mortar in," mutters Dorothy Reynolds as we make our first entrance.

Littler is a round, innocent-looking man who sits bland and expressionless throughout. He laughs once, at a joke about Edward VII. All too soon the boys realise he is not laughing, and they begin to giggle. This is what always used to happen on a bad night of *Beyond the Fringe*: the laughter on stage was inversely proportional to that from the audience. John G. struggles under a heavy cold, his eyes swollen and racked by sneezes, while the Assistant Stage Manager follows him round with a box of Kleenex. It worries me that we open in Manchester in three days and he is still a long way from knowing his words.

SEPTEMBER 30TH. PALACE THEATRE, MANCHESTER
The Palace turns out to be a cavernous theatre, far bigger than my worst imaginings. It has been closed all summer and we are to re-open it. "You won't fill this place," the stage doorman says to Gielgud. "*Ken Dodd* doesn't fill this place." In the afternoon we have a disastrous technical rehearsal with a few actors from Michael Elliott's 69 Theatre in the audience. They laugh a lot in the first half then fall silent. I presume they have left and it is only when the house lights go up that I see they are still there: it's just that they have stopped laughing. I go out before the first performance and find George Fenton and Roger Brain, the horn-player, elbow deep in muck, rubbing their rugger boots up and down the streaming gutter in the pouring rain. Julia Oman had thought they looked too new. Waiting for the curtain, I talk to Mac, John G.'s dresser. He is in his eighties and was dresser to

another Sir John (Martin-Harvey) and before that to Fred Terry. Gielgud rises splendidly to the presence of our first audience, but we all feel lost in this barn of a theatre. The doorman had been right: even on a first night it's less than a third full. And again the same thing happens: halfway through the second act we lose the audience.

OCTOBER 4TH. MANCHESTER
John G. is still far from knowing his words. The opening speech is full of names. He often confuses these and the boys are called by masters' names, masters by boys'. Though he never actually stops and audible prompts are rare, it must leave the audience with a peculiar impression of the play. I *think*. The truth is an audience accepts whatever it sees on the stage as meant. Though an audible prompt embarrasses and withers any laughs in the immediate vicinity, provided one can just keep going an audience will assume everything is as it should be. What is surprising about John G. is that even when it is plain to the audience that he has forgotten his words, the last person to be embarrassed is him. He treats this fortnight in Manchester like an open rehearsal to which the audience is admitted by courtesy. If the show isn't all it should be, that is their look-out. I don't agree with this, but when the curtain goes up night after night on only thirty or forty people, I begin to think he's right. And even with such sparse audiences it's noticeable that if they like him and laugh at his jokes then his confidence grows and his memory improves. But this first week has been very rough and on one evening he so far loses his nerve that he begins the play addressing the boys with his back to the audience. Tonight my parents come. They have obviously been a bit mystified by the play, and sit in my dressing room in awkward silence as my dresser, a veteran of the music halls, puts away my stuff. After he's gone, it transpires they thought *he* was Sir John Gielgud and was ignoring them deliberately because he was unhappy with the play.

OCTOBER 9TH. MANCHESTER
Supper with Sidney Bernstein★ in his penthouse on top of Granada TV. J. G., Patrick, Denis Forman† and Gordon

★ Lord Bernstein (b. 1899), President Granada TV.
† Sir Denis Forman (b. 1917), Chairman, Granada TV.

McDougall★. A nice Mark Gertler, some silver in a bureau and lots of what look like steakhouse Turners but I'm sure aren't. A lovely Gielgud remark: he asks me whether I couldn't write a Noël Coward parody for the second act: "You know the sort of thing, lots of little epigrams, smart witty remarks. It wouldn't be at all difficult."

"I couldn't possibly."

"Why not? It's terribly easy. Noël does it all the time."

It is after midnight when they begin to talk seriously about What Must Be Done With The Play. To start with they have seen it on a depressing night, and Sidney Bernstein, though kind and charming, is slightly deaf, and hasn't caught all the dialogue. He also has the defect, peculiar to high television executives and editors of popular newspapers, of thinking the public stupider than it is. He doesn't think the Bloomsbury parody will work, for instance, because nobody will have heard of Virginia Woolf. Denis Forman, however, makes one valuable suggestion, which we later adopt, namely that the Headmaster should formally take his leave at the end. John G. is still anxious about the opening.

"All that terrible organ music, the slow march and the hymns. Oh, those hymns," he wails. "It's just like school."

"But it *is* school."

"Oh yes. I suppose it is."

They talk on until three in the morning, but by half past two I can stand it no longer and walk out. The cardinal rule in such circumstances is to be sure beforehand that one's exit is clear. Mine isn't, as I don't have a key to the executive lift. I hang about in the lobby feeling foolish until Denis stumps out after me and we go awkwardly down through the dark and empty building, and I walk back to the Midland through the wet streets of Manchester.

OCTOBER 11TH. MANCHESTER
A group of the boys have written a pop song on themes arising out of the play and in gaps of rehearsal they orchestrate it with the help of Carl Davis. This afternoon they sing it over to me, George Fenton and Anthony Andrews singing in high altos above the guitar and organ accompaniment: "In a boater, in a bowler, in a boat, We were drifting away, Never expecting the day, When we wouldn't have our tailors, our servants and our

★ B. 1941, theatre director. Founded Stables Theatre, Manchester, 1969.

sailors, And our old boys playing cricket on the green." I sit in the Tea Centre in Manchester's Oxford Road, working on the lyrics with George Fenton and Keith McNally, and I see suddenly how I shall look back on this time as very happy.

OCTOBER 15TH. THEATRE ROYAL, BRIGHTON
All the time we were in Manchester, the management would encourage us by holding out the prospect of Brighton . . . glittering, sophisticated, metropolitan audiences in a bandbox of a theatre, an ideal setting for a play like ours. I was sceptical. I had been here before in 1961 with *Beyond the Fringe*. It was the week before we went to London, and we played to a handful of old ladies, most of whom had left by the interval: the seats were going up like pistol shots throughout the performance. Brighton is a difficult place to play and can make or mar a production, infested as it is with theatricals who offer advice and scent disaster. "We loved it, darlings," they told us in 1961, "but don't, whatever you do, take it in." However, the first night is good, the audience solid and responsive and the next day we have a perceptive notice from the Brighton critic, Jack Tinker.★ After the performance Diana Cooper,† Enid Bagnold⁰ and T. C. Worsley˟ come round, with Worsley being especially helpful. It is odd to see Diana Cooper standing in my dressing room, friend and contemporary of figures who are legends to me. She had apparently been in tears during Gielgud's memoir of the Lost Generation, an imaginary visit to a country house on the eve of the First World War. "How did you know to choose all those names?" she asks vaguely, eyeing herself in the glass. "They were all my lovers."

At last we seem to be coming out of the wood and producing the sort of reaction we have been after, the transition from nostalgia and genuine regret to laughter and back again, without the one destroying the other.

OCTOBER 19TH. BRIGHTON
The boys are a problem. If they are too rigidly disciplined then they lose the spontaneity that is part of the charm of the play.

★ Jack Tinker (b. 1938), now drama critic of the *Daily Mail*.
† Lady Diana Cooper (b. 1892), former actress (*The Miracle*). Widow of Lord Norwich (Duff Cooper), politician, diplomat and author.
⁰ Enid Bagnold (1889–1981), playwright (*The Chalk Garden*).
˟ T. C. Worsley (1907–77), drama critic of the *Financial Times*.

More experienced actors would counterfeit spontaneity but these can't. So every night they whisper, fight and fart, behave in fact like a classful of kids. To an actor with a speech to make this is a nightmare, as the attention of the audience is subject to constant distraction. Few leading actors would risk this, let alone put up with it, but it never bothers Gielgud. He is completely confident of his ability to hold the stage and the attention. What is going on behind him he treats as an irrelevance. The result is we get the best of both worlds. As for talking directly to the audience there is now no stopping him. He leans far out over the footlights, shading his eyes with his mortar board, ostensibly searching for his straitlaced sister Nancy, but in reality seeing whether there's anyone in that he knows. Audiences who have grown accustomed to him as a somewhat remote and awesome presence obviously find the change delightful. He even starts waving.

He completely lacks pretension. The most moving and magical part of the play is the visit to the country house at the end of the first act. John G. is off stage at the start of this scene, and as like as not in the middle of a story. He tears himself away from the joke, steps out on to the stage, and within seconds he is wreathed in tears, and the audience is in the palm of his hand. The curtain comes down and he turns round and finishes the story. He is not a sentimental man.

After the Saturday matinée I bump into Cyril Connolly★ coming in at the stage door. I have never met him before and assume he is going to see John. "No. It is you I want to see. I want to show you how tall I am." He is referring to a passage in the memoir of Virginia Woolf. "She was one of the tallest writers I have ever known. Which is not to say that her stories were tall. They were not; they were short. But she did stand head and shoulders above her contemporaries, and sometimes of course much more so. Cyril Connolly, for instance, a man of great literary stature only came up to her waist. And sometimes not even there." It is Connolly's own descriptions of himself in *The Unquiet Grave* that have led me into error. I promise to change it (to Dylan Thomas) but I think he's slightly disappointed. He'd rather have me keep his name and change the joke.

★ Cyril Connolly (1903–74), author (*Enemies of Promise*) and literary critic on the *Sunday Times*.

OCTOBER 30TH. APOLLO THEATRE, SHAFTESBURY AVENUE
Noël Coward comes to the final preview. After the performance
I hear his party announced at the stage door and they disappear
into John G.'s dressing-room. It has been a charity show, the
audience very quiet as they invariably are when they have paid
too much for their seats (curiously, if they pay nothing at all the
effect is the same). I sit in my room hoping Coward has liked it
and that if he hasn't he'll have the tact not to show it. Any
criticism or even advice at this late date is destructive. And I
remember the story of Gielgud rehearsing a speech in an empty
theatre, the only other person there a charwoman mopping the
stage. At the finish she is reputed to have leaned on her mop and
said, "I don't think you should do it like that, dear." "Really? Oh
God, how do you think I should do it?" John G. sends Mac to
fetch me in to meet Coward, who is brimming with enthusiasm
and saying all the right things. John is standing there in his shirt
tails with Mac waiting to slip on the knightly trousers, a ritual I
am sure John indulges him in out of the kindness of his heart: to
be helped into one's trousers is no help at all. Meanwhile Coward
is recalling his favourite moments and John is glowing with
pleasure. Though I don't know it at the time, this is going to be
the pattern for this moment in the day for the next twelve
months. Manchester seems a long way away.

NOVEMBER 10TH. REMEMBRANCE DAY
In the first week the play has broken all box-office records and is
an assured success. John G. is very happy and in wonderful form.
I listen to the BBC critics. They all say it is very funny, but what
is it about, what am I trying to do, is there a message? Nobody
knows, least of all me. If one could answer these questions in any
other way than by writing what one has written there would be
no point in writing at all.

Today is Armistice Day and the fiftieth anniversary of the end
of the First World War. I listen to the ceremony on the radio and
as I type this I hear the guns rumbling across the park for the start
of the Two Minutes Silence. I find the ceremony ridiculous and
hypocritical and yet it brings a lump to my throat. Why? I
suppose that is what the play is trying to resolve.

# MICHAEL
# COVENEY

# MICHAEL COVENEY

Michael Coveney (b. 1948) belongs to the younger generation of drama critics. He was editor of *Plays and Players* and is now the reviewer for the *Financial Times*. By the time he first saw Gielgud (in *Ivanov* in 1965) the actor was already a legendary theatrical figure.

# MICHAEL COVENEY

On the last Saturday of February 1976, the National Theatre said goodbye to the Old Vic, a curious conglomerate of theatre notables paying a somewhat limp tribute to Lilian Baylis. Albert Finney looked ill at ease in a velvet dinner jacket. Flora Robson was in tears. Ralph Richardson decorated the great speech of Enobarbus with a cordial string of impenetrable anecdotes, most of them concerning the addiction of Harcourt "Billy" Williams to Bemax. Robert Eddison camped around. Susan Fleetwood smiled gamely, Frank Finlay looked lost. Sybil Thorndike, making, as it turned out, her last appearance in public, rose on her sticks in the stalls to be cheered from the stage.

Then Finney announced Gielgud. He entered upstage left in immaculate evening dress, making for centre stage with quick, foreshortened steps, beaming the while as the light bounced ecstatically around that noble, glistening dome. To say he was bald would be too bald a thing to say. He stood basking rhapsodically in an ovation that tumbled, wave upon wave, throughout the house and broke in a crashing spume at the recipient's feet. Gielgud, never a King Canute of the theatre, stood to attention and allowed himself a dignified, well-earned paddle. He blubbed a little.

Eventually, silence and stillness. Then he launched, at top speed and with stunningly perfect articulation, into Hamlet's "Oh, what a rogue and peasant slave" soliloquy. If, there and then, the Old Vic had announced a revival with Gielgud in the part he has played over 500 times but not for thirty-seven years I would have parked myself that night on the pavement of the Waterloo Road and waited for the box office to open.

For one brief shining moment we were there in Camelot. No doubt, for many in the audience, this was how Shakespeare should be spoken. Kenneth Tynan once paid Gielgud the backhanded compliment of being "the finest actor on earth from the neck up", which is rather like saying it's all very well for Isaac Stern to play his Stradivarius but, my dear, he really should try and wiggle those hips more often.

He has never been the athlete, the Olivieresque panther preferred by Tynan. He is a calm and methodical virtuoso in a world full of people wiggling their hips. From his toes to his pate, Gielgud is the actor as vocal instrument par excellence. But anyone who believes that liquid gold gushes in a molten stream from the larynx unaided by anything less than total, albeit invisible, physical effort, knows nothing of how the body, or indeed an opera singer, works.

All actors have their heroes. Many today cite the example and influence of Olivier, of Williamson, of Brando, of Steiger, or of Finney. Gielgud, however, although much imitated around dinner tables and in green rooms, is in fact inimitable. He is a glorious one-off. He may seem, at a superficial level, to represent a vanished tradition, but I think this is a myth-laden way of trying to explain his uniqueness. The actors he himself most admired in his youth were Claude Rains (his teacher at RADA), Noël Coward (whom he succeeded in *The Vortex* and *The Constant Nymph* in the mid-twenties) and Leslie Faber. And then again he knew at first hand of the great actor-managers such as Fred Terry (his great-uncle), Sir John Martin-Harvey, Matheson Lang and Robert Loraine.

We know that he first thought of being a stage designer, impressed as he was by the work of his second cousin Gordon Craig. And his entry into the theatre was undoubtedly smoothed by family connections; he was engaged for the first time as a touring stage manager and understudy by his cousin Phyllis Neilson-Terry. He was impressed by the work of such directors as Granville-Barker and Komisarjevsky.

But the theatre is an immediate, pragmatic art, and Gielgud's reminiscences have often proved a red herring in the sensible evaluation of his contribution. He may well have found his true ambience in the protected, privileged world of Binkie

Beaumont's* West End, but my own experience has been one of fascinated appreciation of how this remarkable actor has adapted his talent to the changing theatre around him, despite all those self-confessedly hasty remarks about Beckett and Brecht.

I did not get off to a good start with his Ivanov at the Phoenix in 1965. It drove me mad. I scribbled an angry adolescent poem the minute I got home: "Ivanov, Ivanov, we've all had enough of your whimpering, simpering whine. Your tiresome self-pity is not even witty . . ." and here, thank God, the memory gives up.

What really first aroused my interest was his performance in 1968 as the Headmaster in Alan Bennett's *Forty Years On*. Befuddled, wispy, absurdly authoritarian, regretful and funny, Gielgud's portrayal was a knowing lament for a vanished era in both education and British life at large, brilliantly and sympathetically fuelled by Bennett's limpid, graceful prose. "The crowd has found the door into the secret garden," was the final sentence in a speech of sudden perception. The world was rushing by.

And, as it rushed, Gielgud found a new lease of life in acknowledging the fact. Six years later he was at the Royal Court playing Shakespeare in Edward Bond's *Bingo* (an apotheosis devoutly not to be wished, in some quarters) with a different, though comparable, sense of beached isolation. Bond's Bard, in a sort of Marxist bondbardment, is a writer living his final days off the fat of the land he has cynically consigned to the socially evil consequences of the enclosures. Drunk and despairing, he finds himself exiled in a landscape of white, white snow:

> I didn't want to die. I could lie in this snow a whole life. I can think now, the thoughts come so easily over the snow and under my shroud. New worlds. Keys turning new locks – pushing iron open like lion's teeth. Wolves will drag me through the snow. I'll sit in their lair and smile and be rich. In the morning or when I die the sun will rise and melt it all away. The dream. The wolves. The iron teeth. The snow. The wind. My voice. A dream that leads to sleep.

As they say in *Forty Years On* when the Headmaster is caught up in a school play of which he is deeply, and rightly, suspicious, this is all a far cry from *Dear Octopus*. In both Bennett and Bond,

* Hugh "Binkie" Beaumont (1908–73), impresario; Managing Director H. M. Tennent Ltd under whose aegis Gielgud often acted and directed.

Gielgud, perhaps fortuitously, came across texts that energised his obvious gift for nostalgia, for wrapping himself in a blanket against the icy winds of change. The blanket, however, was electric.

*Bingo* had first been presented at the Northcott Theatre in Exeter, and Bond purists were understandably troubled by the fact that Gielgud's presence in the Royal Court revival made the dramatist suddenly and overwhelmingly popular at the box office. Despite the obvious attractions in the role for Gielgud, I nonetheless feel that his involvement in a play of which he was very probably nervous was a far greater risk than that taken by Olivier with *The Entertainer.*

The real difference lies in the fact that Olivier's career usually progressed as a series of low-risk calculations, whereas Gielgud has gone along good-naturedly with the tide. In a book of essays published in 1981 to celebrate the twenty-fifth anniversary of the English Stage Company at the Royal Court, Gielgud avoids any mention of *Bingo*, praising rather the opportunity first offered him in Sloane Square in 1970 by David Storey's *Home* in a production by Lindsay Anderson.

*Home* was a peculiar, evanescent play, set, it eventually transpires, in a lunatic asylum, where Gielgud and his old friend Richardson talked random gibberish and transformed it by their art. ("The past. It conjures up some images.") Gielgud has always been a famed weeper on stage, and suddenly you noticed, as if someone had pulled an invisible cord, his eyes filling with tears. These odd moments of incontinent emotionalism invested the evening with a worrying, furtive sort of intensity. The tears traced slowly across a pointilliste tapestry of old age and seclusion, a hymn to the island race and a vague hint of irregularities involving small girls. One felt Storey had written for the actors in a way younger actors are rarely written for these days. What poignant irony when Gielgud deflected in Dandy Nichols' direction the regretful sigh, "No great role for this actor, I'm afraid. A little stage, a tiny part."

And what artistry, what a double act, Gielgud and Richardson together in the sunset glow of their careers, dismissing tartly the passing parade of fellow inmates, lamenting the past, sparring in the present and oblivious to the future. Richardson's idiosyncratic dapperness seems always to be a consciously cultivated characteristic, whereas Gielgud effortlessly emanates style, polish, assurance. You see old men like Richardson walking briskly along the sea front in Eastbourne or Hove. But you cannot put a postmark on Gielgud's brand of seigneurial old age. The wonderful paradox is that Gielgud, a monarch in exile from a distant theatrical and social élite, is ideally and mysteriously equipped to play the role of an aloof participant in the suburban meandering of a theatre that both adores and mistrusts him.

Two years after *Home* at the Royal Court, he played Sir Geoffrey Kendle in Charles Wood's *Veterans*, a part that seemed even more deliberately tailored to what we know of him: Sir Geoffrey was prone to fits of devastating but quite unintentional tactlessness. Everyone has his own stock of Gielgud stories, and no living actor is more encrusted with the affectionate barnacles of apocrypha than he.

While appearing in *Forty Years On* he directed *Don Giovanni* for the newly formed English National Opera at the Coliseum. I heard that he was having trouble one day with the placement of an extra on stage during the course of a final rehearsal. The orchestra was in full majestic flow when Gielgud noticed this sadly wandering offender at the back of a crowd. Unable to attract his attention, he burst down the centre aisle, arms waving, and shouted at the conductor "Stop, oh stop, that terrible music!"

The Edward Knoblock and Athene Seyler stories abound, of course, but my own especial favourite concerns a senior, rather dull supporting actor (now dead) whom we shall call Miles Thornton. For weeks Thornton had been on tour with Gielgud and had received not one word, of abuse, encouragement or even greeting, from his by now terrifying colleague. Eventually the pressure was too much and the bemused thespian took his courage in both hands and, in one of the large provincial towns, stood trembling outside the Number One dressing room. He knocked, tentatively, just before the half was called. "Come," cried Gielgud from within and, on seeing a vaguely familiar profile edging round the door, expostulated, "My dear boy, thank heavens it's you. For one dreadful moment I thought it was going to be that ghastly old bore Miles Thornton."

If I do our subject a disservice I can only claim in my defence that many of *his* stories, delightedly recounted in legend and in print, are equally apocryphal. I have had occasion to check one or two about Ingrid Bergman ("Dear Ingrid – speaks five languages and can't act in any of them") and find them rooted in fact but flamboyantly elaborated for effect.

Harold Pinter's *No Man's Land* in 1975 was the second great contemporary idyll for the old firm of Gielgud and Richardson. Gielgud was a benign old poet, a supplicant in a Regent's Park drawing room amazingly transformed to an approximate likeness of W. H. Auden: his hair strayed carelessly down to his right eyebrow, a stained tie flapped above a most un-Gielgudian bulging stomach. The image was completed by the shabby grey suit with thin stripes too widely spaced for any hint of respectability, and the evocatively slovenly footwear of socks and open-toed sandals. Gielgud has never been known for disguising himself, but not even his black, conquistadorial Othello, or that funny-looking Lear in an absurdly ferocious Japanese wig-cum-beard, could have been more drastic exercises in self-immolation.

Pinter's idyll was more apocalyptic than Storey's, more brilliantly written, certainly more alcoholic. Gielgud played Spooner, the fading literato who has bumped into Richardson in a famed North London pub, Jack Straw's Castle. After a baroque preamble of ingratiating subservience – like Eliot's Prufrock, Spooner is "deferential, glad to be of use, politic, cautious and meticulous" – Gielgud switched syntactic gear to gain a most wonderful first big laugh: "Do you often hang about Hampstead Heath?"

Comment at the time tended to emphasise the extraordinary physical coups executed by Richardson as he leapt at the curtains to pull them savagely shut or dived to the floor in a frighteningly unpremeditated cataleptic fit. But, as in *Home*, this was an equal match of contrasting temperaments, with Gielgud coming to elegiac rest in a room where he feels he might be safe at last. His long protestations of devotion, expertly phrased, are cruelly ignored by Richardson, but still Gielgud/Spooner takes comfort in memories – of the English language, of bucolic life, of grandchildren. Again, the past is a matter for poignant regret, "What happened to our cottages, what happened to our lawns?" But you have to be aware of the present in order to successfully negotiate the pull of the past. In other words, you have to know what you are doing.

The idea, therefore, that Gielgud has shambled reluctantly into the contemporary theatre is entirely fallacious. When the small theatre of the National on the South Bank, the Cottesloe, opened in March 1977, the first show was Ken Campbell's racy sci-fi epic *Illuminatus!*, in which the conspiracy theory was given full wacky rein in a series of rough theatre antics spread over five plays and eight hours. In a stroke of casting rivalled for wittiness only by the same company's assignation of God to Brian Glover in the *Mystery Plays*, Gielgud played the recorded voice of a speaking computer, hired, at the end, to apply soothing balm to the open wounds of a crazy narrative.

Anyone of my generation, born since the last war, has obviously missed the great years of Gielgud in Shakespeare. But his Prospero for the National at the Old Vic in 1974 was both a glimpse of the past and a thoroughly alive interpretation. This was also the year of Bond's *Bingo*, and a colleague, Peter Ansorge, interestingly speculated that Gielgud's Prospero presented "the magician as an explorer of the possibilities and limits of art . . . the fact that the imagination of order is by no means a reflection of its actual presence in life." Peter Hall's production, too, made a fascinating statement about the moment in theatrical history when artificial moons, storms and masques became a practical proposition for producers and playwrights.

This was an undervalued, experimental production of *The Tempest* that would have been unthinkable without the very special resonances Gielgud brought to his role. The same willingness to exploit his unique status in the British theatre was apparent in an otherwise lacklustre revival by John Schlesinger of *Julius Caesar* at the National in 1977. One or two critics unkindly suggested that the assassination was the result of a plot to kill off the best verse speaker in the English language. But even after death, this Caesar, through a series of production tricks and ornaments, continued to dominate the play in a way no other Caesar of my experience has accomplished.

The Olivier stage was bedecked with images of Gielgud's countenance, disapproval crinkling imperiously around his splendid nose, as if what the new democracy got up to was nothing to do with him and pretty despicable even if it was.

Although Gielgud on the contemporary stage has continually celebrated the past and old values, his voice has never been above charting, in its endless variety of nuance and inflection, the mood of the present.

The "secret garden" speech in Bennett's *Forty Years On* is a fair summary of how Gielgud has been creatively trapped, with a song in his heart, between the jostling claims of today and yesterday.

> Once we had a romantic and old-fashioned conception of honour, of patriotism, chivalry and duty. But it was a duty which didn't have much to do with justice, with social justice anyway. And in default of that justice and in pursuit of it, that was how the great words came to be cancelled out.

The fact remains that much of what is of value in today's theatre exists because of the astonishingly relentless careers of Gielgud, Richardson and Olivier. The heirs apparent in the post-war theatre – Burton, O'Toole, Finney – were easily seduced from total commitment to the stage by the lure of Hollywood and the spurious trappings of modern stardom. Today, a young actor has hardly played Hamlet for the first time, or Lear for a few weeks, before he buries his classical theatre ambitions and makes a TV series, a film in Spain, a lurid thriller in Tinsel Town.

The old stars visit these scenarios from time to time, and quickly carve an unforgettable cameo. But that one brief shining moment at the Old Vic eight years ago gave me, at least, a taste of incomparable, unforgettable, hard-won magic. To his eternal credit, Gielgud has refused to rest on his laurels and has entered into the confusing hurlyburly of the modern theatre with great spirit, an open mind, and a generous heart. He has maintained a creative presence there not only with ineradicable dignity, but also with the humility which is the hallmark of only the best of men.

# DEREK
# GRANGER

## DEREK GRANGER

Derek Granger (b. 1921) was a drama critic and a literary editor before becoming a distinguished producer of television programmes. In 1981 he produced for Granada Television Evelyn Waugh's novel, *Brideshead Revisited*, which was highly acclaimed on both sides of the Atlantic. John Gielgud was cast as Edward Ryder.

# DEREK GRANGER

I first saw John Gielgud's unforgettable Hamlet on a sweltering night in Singapore just before the onset of the monsoon season. The year was 1945 and I was then, much to my continuing surprise, the navigator of a clumsy-looking naval vessel called a Landing Ship Tank. We had sailed three months previously en route for the far-eastern theatre of war and an eventual seaborne landing upon the Japanese mainland. Now in Singapore harbour we were awaiting new sailing instructions for Bangkok. The atom bomb had fallen on Hiroshima and our own prospective contribution to the assault on Japan had become quite suddenly superfluous.

As with many a sailor at that time Cyril Connolly's *The Unquiet Grave* was on my bunkside shelf, hoarded copies of *Horizon* were crammed in my kitbag and *Swann's Way* was lights-out reading in the cradle of the deep so I therefore attended the first night of *Hamlet* as member of a special shore-leave party in a mood of rare expectation. After months of being steeped in no other language than the cheerful vernacular of fo'c'sle and quarterdeck the prospect of hearing "the tongue that Shakespeare spake" uttered in the cello-like tones of the most eloquent actor of the English theatre seemed a precious and unlikely boon. The Vasco da Gama side of me – for I had learned by laborious rule-of-thumb to plot a course by star-sight and was now deeply in thrall to the mysteries of celestial navigation – was firmly suppressed on that stifling night in favour of the culture-hungry aesthete. Our party had acquired privileged seats immediately behind the heavily gold-braided staff of the Supreme East Asia Allied Command who were now ranked on either side of the noble, if slightly distracting, head of Supremo himself – Admiral of the Fleet Lord Louis Mountbatten. Yet in spite of that awesome weight of attendant top brass, the whirring of the fans, the dusty black drapes which served as scenery, the miasmic tropical heat-haze which seemed to have enveloped the entire far-eastern war-base, in spite of all these improbable circumstances of time and place, there was no doubt that here was something marvellous – in steamy Singapore, of all improbable places, I was watching the definitive poet-philosopher Hamlet of our century.

I did not meet John Gielgud then but I did briefly meet his Ophelia, the haunting and lovely Hazel Terry, who was later to become a close friend. She had once been described by Harold Hobson as "beautiful as a galleon and twice as large". Hazel was also one of the most lovable, witty and understanding of women, blessed in abundance with that rarest of qualities, the gift of intimate companionship.

I first met John three years later one mid-summer morning on the Brighton sea front. He was walking with David Webster, the administrator of Covent Garden who spent his weekends in a resplendent seaside flat in Kemp Town. John was then directing *The Glass Menagerie*, the first play by Tennessee Williams to be produced in England. It had opened the night before at the Theatre Royal, Brighton, and I had reviewed it in that morning's *Sussex Daily News*. This was in my new post-war capacity as general dogsbody on the two local newspapers, the *Sussex Daily News* and *Evening Argus*. Together with my old friend and colleague, Peter Black, who was then reviewing theatre for the *Argus*, I had found an agreeable way of cutting my critical teeth. This was at the time when almost every West End play of any importance opened in Brighton, particularly the star-studded and lavish productions of H. M. Tennent. Because Peter and I were the first reviewers ever to commit our opinion to print we had acquired a small reputation, though both of us believed the accounts of our critical acumen were greatly exaggerated.

I was diffident then about meeting the actors and others whose work I had to assess professionally, but it never seemed to make any difference to them and friendships formed in the little backstage bar of the Theatre Royal ("The Single Gulp") with people of the theatre such as Oliver Messel, Terence Rattigan, Peter Glenville, Frith Banbury and Robert Flemyng have endured for a lifetime. At John's beautiful small eighteenth-century house in Cowley Street (a more fitting habitation for him could hardly be imagined) there were memorable dinner parties which nicely combined splendid food and company and always much laughter. In return there were kitchen suppers in my attic flat in Gloucester Place, and over the years, meetings and parties with many mutual friends. There were also later encounters in New York (I remember Bernie, John's endearingly neurotic servant, nudging me in a dark Greenwich Village cabaret to announce a party on the West Side). I dwell a little on these personal reminiscences because it has taken Anthony Powell's *A Dance to the Music of Time* to persuade us how these intricate webs of friendship and acquaintance are spun in all our lives, often through the most surprising agencies of chance and coincidence. It is not until years later that we discern the fascinating patterns that they make and learn how everything seems finally to converge.

I saw John last in Piccadilly, just before I started on this memoir. With typical energy he was on his way from an art show in Cork Street and was now stopping for a short pause at Hatchards before setting off to see the latest film. As always I felt a sharp stab of self-criticism as that immaculately elegant figure hove into view. I have never seen him, not even in rehearsal, appear otherwise than as "the glass of fashion and the mould of form". Such unvarying and enviable spruceness has the effect of making me feel like a rather carelessly wrapped parcel. After counting up, I believe I have seen over thirty of John's performances. From the time I was a schoolboy and first saw him as a vividly intense young Romeo in Michel Saint-Denis' famous production with Peggy Ashcroft and Laurence Olivier (I can still recall the details after almost fifty years) I have been able to watch a contribution to the art of acting which has been one of the glories of twentieth-century theatre. Not in theatrical history has there been a contemporaneous trio to match Olivier, Richardson and Gielgud. A particularly godsent aspect of this extraordinary triumvirate is that in each of their long careers, now over half a century, they have been not rivals but richly representative talents in a great arc or spectrum of human types. If Olivier is the king, the lion, the god, the hero and sometimes the black villain of the trio (Oedipus, Henry V, Richard III); if Richardson is the transmuted stuff of ordinary clay with a pipeline to the dreams and longings of the common man (Peer Gynt, Falstaff, Cyrano and the "little man" heroes of Priestley and Sherriff); then John is supremely the prince, the poet and philosopher, the aesthete and the dandy (Richard II, Prospero, Valentine, Benedick, Jack Worthing). If Olivier is fire, thunder, animal magnetism and danger; if Richardson is bemused wonder, slyness, and compassion; then John is poetic sensibility, philosophical introspection, detachment, reason, quicksilver wit and everything that is expressive of an intense inner life.

At the very beginnings of his career a range of parts quickly established his ascendancy in a certain kind of role. Shakespeare's (and Gordon Daviot's) Richard II, the abject self-analysing philosopher-king was the epitome of that character in its most tragic form; Prospero the most pensive, subtle and inward-looking; and the long line of sensitives, gadabouts and dandies which followed – Valentine in *Love For Love*, Joseph Surface in *The School For Scandal*, Benedick in *Much Ado*, Jack Worthing in *The Importance Of Being Earnest* – exemplified the frivolous and comic side of that amalgam, all of them models of the utmost grace, finish and style. Allied to the cadences of the most beautiful voice in the English theatre was a bearing and manner of equal eloquence. If there is one image of him which one holds in the mind's eye it must surely be something very close to Nicholas Hilliard's exquisite Elizabethan miniature of the languid gallant posed against the rose tree.

There have been two turning points in this long and splendidly strenuous career. The first was when Peter Brook brilliantly cast him as Angelo in *Measure For Measure* at Stratford in 1950. This production, in its incisiveness and insight, set a new standard for modern Shakespearean production and enabled John to discover within Angelo a dark and chilling urgency which froze the blood. This was to become a new blade in his actor's armoury and his rancorous Cassius in the film of *Julius Caesar* and his grimly impassioned Leontes in Brook's *A Winter's Tale* continued to show him exploiting a new vein of mastery.

The second moment of late revelation was his ancient Headmaster in Alan Bennett's *Forty Years On* in which he suddenly emerged as the most wonderfully ripe actor of comedy with a marvellous line in rich buffoonery. His development into a great comic player has provided one of the staple delights of cinema and television audiences across the world. A brilliantly funny Gielgud cameo has come to seem an obligatory requirement for any aspiring television series or major international film.

John has always been one of the most modest of our leading actors. If it is a modesty which properly contains a sure sense of his own worth, his personality lacks all trace of self-advertisement. I have often been told that when appearing in one of his own productions he will tend to neglect himself, preferring to guide and help his fellow players in his role as director. Perhaps the aristocratic-bohemian lineage of his Terry ancestry accounts for a kind of inner confidence which can dispense with the debilitating wear and tear of ambition. For all his quiet assurance he seems immensely uncompetitive. In fact a much greater part of his career than most of us acknowledge has been devoted to bringing out the best in others as a most zealous and meticulous stage director. Few actors are usually so outward-looking in their other interests, or so discerning in their taste, or read so much, look at so much painting, listen to so much music, or see so much in the theatre and cinema. There seems in his make-up a streak which for an actor seems curiously unexpected – detachment.

When recently I told him I was coming to see him in his latest London play it was not surprising to hear him urging me to see it quickly before a fellow actor, whose performance was much delighting him, left the cast.

It is indicative that he should have announced his belief that bad notices teach one more than good and that failure tends to be more interesting than success. For an actor these are sentiments which argue the rarest kind of dispassionate curiosity. The vein of detachment has also given a unique quality to his interpretation of character; his portraits of Hamlet and Richard II, of Benedick and Angelo, are marked by acute insight and carry a sense of worldly understanding that cuts deep into the imagination. That is why one now looks forward to a last superb Winter-flowering Prospero in which the essence of late Shakespearean poetry and wisdom will find again its most perfect and sonorous interpreter.

I first worked with John in 1978 as the producer of the Granada Television version of *No Man's Land*. This was not a particularly onerous assignment for me as it consisted simply of ensuring that the remarkable National Theatre stage production, directed by

Sir Peter Hall, was transferred to the television screen more or less intact. It was a joy, however, to watch John and Sir Ralph Richardson working together, friends and colleagues for fifty years, each now so beautifully attuned to the other's temperament and technique that it was like watching a duet by two instrumentalists who had practised together for a lifetime. John's portrait of the seedy poet-tasting Spooner will endure as one of his most unforgettable comic creations. Spooner's physical appearance – a wonder of slept-in dishevelment – had been slyly modelled on a famous and venerated modern poet and it added immensely to the feeling that this was no character plucked from the imagination but one drawn vividly from life. At the end of the play there is a speech, at least a thousand words long, in which poor Spooner entreats his enigmatic and tyrannical host (played by Sir Ralph) for a permanent position in his household. There was, inevitably, a slight tremor of tension in the studio before this important "take". It was obviously essential to complete it in one single shot and as John bravely awaited his cue the studio stilled as he embarked on this verbal marathon. When he finished there was a short pause of stunned amazement which suddenly turned into the sound of rapturous appreciation as the entire studio floor let forth a spontaneous roar of applause. John had delivered, without a single fluff, six pages of incredibly complicated monologue, not only letter-perfect but with every stress and inflection, nuance and underlining, every demi-semi quaver miraculously intact.

Two years later we invited him to play Charles Ryder's father in Granada's production of *Brideshead Revisited*. For us there never was any other possibility and we were delighted when John, who had a great personal fondness for Waugh's novel, accepted with every sign of pleasure. Because of our long and difficult schedule we could offer only tentative provisional dates but even these were to be abandoned. For suddenly, in August 1979, our whole huge caravan of a production came to a shuddering stop. One August day in Oxford we were strike-bound and were to remain so for three whole months. We had already spent over a million pounds of our budget and now everything was frozen. All our actors were out of contract; our locations were lost; our first director, Michael Lindsay-Hogg, had to return to honour professional commitments in America; and our planned summer shooting was in total disarray.

Then one day in late October the strike finished as suddenly as it began and once again we were asked to get into production. It was a very faltering new beginning for there was no possible guarantee that we might not founder again, perhaps this time for good. Our complicated schedules had to be improvised from week to week, so now in mid-winter we had no alternative but to start at the end of the novel and, as it were, work our way backwards. But one can never tell when one's luck is running. Charles Sturridge (later to be much described by John as reminding him of the young Peter Brook) joined us as director; most of our cast were ready to be recontracted; and Castle Howard was available and welcoming. We then had a huge stroke of good fortune. We needed all our great guest stars – Laurence Olivier, John Gielgud, Claire Bloom, Stephane Audran – to be immediately available. By some miracle these indefatigable performers, usually en route from one great feature movie to the next, were free to join us. John arrived to join the cast of *Brideshead* at Castle Howard in January 1980. So began a contribution that turned out to be one of the richest and most memorable features of the programme.

With the character of Waugh's Ryder Senior (based partly on the author's father) there was no aspect of patriarchal intimidation which he was to leave unexplored. The remorseless tones of false bonhomie masking a chilly indifference, the pinprick sallies, the deeply unconvivial banter, the heavily feigned concern hiding bleak disinterest – no father could ever have confronted his son in better shape to play the teasing sadist. It was a performance of wickedly comic virtuosity and one which wrung from the wonderfully funny old monster of Waugh's creation every acidulous drop.

John had prepared the part with his usual incisive thoroughness. We had been over the script for several days, checking every line for possible changes and working on small improvements. No performer could be more exemplary when at work. Always punctual, nearly always word-perfect, relaxed and infinitely patient and forbearing over all the inevitable delays, irritations and frustrations of the day-to-day business of filming, his presence on the set is hugely appreciated. In breaks from filming he can become superbly entertaining company as he relaxes often to reminisce with great point and gusto about his long theatrical past. It is not only his fellow actors who enjoy his companionship at such moments; he also has the esteem and warm support of all the crew. There is no one so agreeable to have as a working colleague or one whose influence seems so bracing and beneficial.

Today John seems to have come into a serene and golden autumn. That quality of detachment (the quality of himself which perhaps gave Ryder Senior such a forbidding reality) has served him well. He remains a profound and fastidious artist but one who, seemingly without effort, still continues, as he reaches eighty, to be endlessly creative and surprising. Today he seems to convey a great measure of contentment. One derives from him a sense of someone who has arrived at a destination not only without too great a pang of disappointment but with a positive sense of gratitude. Although he is nearly always working, moving across the world from one film or television location to the next, he prefers when in England to spend nearly all his spare time in his charming country retreat in Buckinghamshire. While I was dining with him in Manchester, just before the last bout of filming on *Brideshead*, he explained how much his life, during breaks from work, was now spent with music and books, reading, playing the gramophone and enjoying the simple and peaceful pleasures of country life. I remonstrated with him over the fact that his friends complained they never saw him, that people were saying he had become reclusive, that he was impossible to get hold of, that he hardly ever went out. "Oh," he replied. "But I've been out."

---

# POSTSCRIPT

# POSTSCRIPT

Dear John,

When we met to discuss this book I remember telling you that I would not let you have a list of prospective contributors for fear you might be offended or hurt in the unlikely event of anyone turning me down. Over the months, I have kept more or less to my resolve but there is one name missing which may cause you to wonder and which, I feel, requires explanation.

I wrote to Ralph Richardson at the same time I wrote to the others. I received no reply. His silence puzzled me but then I learned he was rehearsing a new play, *Inner Voices*, at the National, so decided not to chivvy him until he had opened and settled down. Some weeks later I wrote to him again and received the following reply, dated July 17th, 1983:

> Thanks for your letter just received – & started a reply to say I had NEVER had anything regards John Gielgud's BOOK.
> Few minutes after I found yours of MAY 3rd among some holiday snaps in France – must have received it there and forgotten.
> Will put something to you before AUG. 30th. Am honoured to be asked to contribute.

Some time towards the middle of August he telephoned. "Care to have tea with me on the 23rd?" he asked. Nothing would give me greater pleasure than to have tea with him, I said. "Iced coffee, actually, will that be all right?" I assured him it would and a week later I presented myself at Chester Terrace, on an unbearably close day punctuated by tepid showers. The iced coffee was welcome.

He had not, of course, told me the reason for the invitation, nor was he forthcoming when I first arrived. We talked of this and that, of his early days in the theatre, of his present performance. He was, I thought, being particularly cagey as only he knew how. At last, he said, "This piece for Johnny's eightieth. Made a start. Can't finish. Trouble is can't hold a pen. Something wrong with my hand. Nothing serious. But can't hold the pen. Shall I read you what I've written?"

We made our way up to his study at the top of the house; he sat at his desk, I beside him. "You smoke a pipe, don't you?" he said. "Good. Don't have many pipe-smoking friends any more. Help yourself to some tobacco," and he pushed towards me a beautiful silver tobacco jar which I admired. "Johnny gave me that. He's given me so many things. Gave us some glorious silver for our silver wedding, so that whenever we dine – there's Johnny. He's everywhere in this house. I think of him often. Wonderful actor. Wonderful friend. Never known a man so keen on the theatre. Extraordinary. I've had lunch with Johnny and the moment I mention something that isn't to do with the theatre, he goes blank. Gets that bored look" – a spectacular impersonation of you bored accompanied this – "and so I've taken to saying things on purpose just to get the reaction. The other day I told him Concorde flies faster than sound. On cue, the bored look. Wonderful fellow." He chuckled with enormous pleasure at the memory.

He then produced a file of papers. "About this piece," he said. "When I'm able to continue, just want to be sure it's the sort of thing you want." A good deal of shuffling the papers followed until he found the appropriate place. "Thought I'd begin," he said, "by welcoming Johnny to the Eighty-year-old club. Looked it up in the dictionary. He'll be an octogenarian. Thought I'd use the word. What d'you think?" I said I agreed it would be a good word to use. "Thought I'd go on to say that the Eighty-year-old club wasn't as exclusive as he might think. But he wasn't to worry because, being a year older than him, I'd always be there to welcome him to the Ninety-year-old club. We'd have a table by the window and I'd take him to lunch. Introduce him to his fellow members, d'you see? Membership's a little more exclusive. Then, of course, I'd be waiting to welcome Johnny to the most exclusive club of all: the Hundred-year-old club. Chaps get very foxy when they reach a hundred." He twitched his nose in perfect imitation of a fox. "Very foxy, indeed. Expect Johnny and I'd be about the foxiest fellows there. Well. What d'you think? Sort of thing you're after? Anybody done anything similar?" I assured him it was just the sort of thing I was after, and, no, no one had written anything remotely similar.

Promising he would finish the piece as soon as his hand was better, he insisted on seeing me out into the street. He seemed to me, the trouble with his hand apart, in wonderful spirits: full of sweetness and good cheer. I thanked him for one of the most pleasant afternoons I'd had in years.

September passed and I heard nothing from him. I wrote a gentle reminder. His wife telephoned to say he wasn't well but that he was very anxious to deliver the piece for this book. That was on Friday, October 7th. Three days later he died.

I have set these things down for the record and because I thought you might like to know.

Yours ever,
Ronnie

# A CHRONOLOGY

*The Importance of Being Earnest*, Globe, 1939
caricature by Sheriffs

# JOHN GIELGUD

## Chronological Table of Parts and Productions

**1921**

| Nov | Old Vic | *Henry V* | Herald |

**1922**

| Mar | Old Vic | *Peer Gynt* | Walk on |
| Mar | Old Vic | *King Lear* | Walk on |
| Apr | Old Vic | *Wat Tyler* | Walk on |
| Sept | Tour | *The Wheel* | Lieut. Manners, A.S.M. and understudy |

**1923**

| May | Regent | *The Insect Play* | White Butterfly |
| June | Regent | *Robert E. Lee* | Aide de Camp, understudy |
| Dec | Comedy | *Charley's Aunt* | Charley |

**1924**

| Jan | Oxford Playhouse | *Captain Brassbound's Conversion* | Johnson |
| Jan | Oxford Playhouse | *Love for Love* | Valentine |
| Feb | Oxford Playhouse | *Mr Pim Passes By* | Brian Strange |
| Feb | Oxford Playhouse | *She Stoops to Conquer* | Young Marlow |

| | | | |
|---|---|---|---|
| Feb | Oxford Playhouse | *Monna Vanna* | Prinzevalle |
| Feb | RADA Theatre | *Romeo and Juliet* | Paris |
| May | Regent | *Romeo and Juliet* | Romeo |
| Oct | RADA Players | *The Return Half* | John Sherry |
| Oct | Oxford Playhouse | *Candida* | Marchbanks |
| Oct | Oxford Playhouse | *Deirdre of the Sorrows* | Naisi |
| Nov | Oxford Playhouse | *A Collection will be Made* | Paul Roget |
| Nov | Oxford Playhouse | *Everybody's Husband* | A Domino |
| Nov | Oxford Playhouse | *The Cradle Song* | Antonio |
| Nov | Oxford Playhouse | *John Gabriel Borkman* | Erhart |
| Nov | Oxford Playhouse | *His Widow's Husband* | Zurita |
| Dec | Oxford Playhouse | *Madame Pepita* | Augusto |
| Dec | Film | *Who is the Man?* | Daniel |

**1925**

| | | | |
|---|---|---|---|
| Jan | Oxford Playhouse | *A Collection will be Made* | Paul Roget |
| Jan | Oxford Playhouse | *Smith* | Algernon |
| Jan | Oxford Playhouse | *The Cherry Orchard* | Trofimov |
| Feb | Royalty | *The Vortex* | Understudy |
| Mar | Comedy | *The Vortex* | Understudy; 16 and 17 Mar & 21 Apr Nicky Lancaster |
| Apr | RADA Players (special perf.) | *The Nature of the Evidence* | The lover |
| May | The Little | *The Vortex* | Understudy |
| May | Aldwych (special perf.) | *The Orphan* | Castalio |
| May | Lyric, Hammersmith | *The Cherry Orchard* | Trofimov |
| May | Royalty | *The Cherry Orchard* | Trofimov |
| June | The Little | *The Vortex* | Nicky Lancaster |
| Aug | Oxford Playhouse | *The Lady from the Sea* | A Stranger |
| Aug | Oxford Playhouse | *The Man with a Flower in his Mouth* | Title Part |
| Sept | Apollo (special perf.) | *Two Gentlemen of Verona* | Valentine |
| Oct | The Little | *The Seagull* | Konstantin |
| Oct | New, Oxford (special perf.) | *Dr Faustus* | Good Angel |
| Dec | Prince's (special perf.) | *L'Ecole des Cocottes* | Robert |
| Dec | The Little | *Gloriana* | Sir John Harington |

**1926**

| | | | |
|---|---|---|---|
| Jan | Savoy (matinées) | *The Tempest* | Ferdinand |
| Jan | RADA Players (special perf.) | *Sons and Fathers* | Richard Southern |
| Feb | Barnes Theatre | *Three Sisters* | Tuzenbach |
| Feb | Barnes Theatre | *Katerina* | Georg |
| June | Court | *Hamlet* | Rosencrantz |
| July | Garrick (special perf.) | *The Lady of the Camellias* | Armand |
| July | Court (300 Club) | *Confession* | Wilfred Marlay |
| Oct | New | *The Constant Nymph* | Lewis Dodd |

**1927**

| | | | |
|---|---|---|---|
| Apr | Apollo (special perf.) | *Othello* | Cassio |
| June | Strand (special perf.) | *The Great God Brown* | Dion Anthony |
| Aug | Tour | *The Constant Nymph* | Lewis Dodd |

**1928**

| | | | |
|---|---|---|---|
| Jan | Majestic, New York | *The Patriot* | The Tsarevich |
| Mar | Wyndham's (matinées) | *Ghosts* | Oswald |
| Apr | Arts | *Ghosts* | Oswald |
| June | Arts (matinées) | *Prejudice* | Jacob Slovak |
| June | Globe | *Holding out the Apple* | Dr Gerald Marlowe |
| Aug | Shaftesbury | *The Skull* | Captain Allenby |
| Oct | Court | *The Lady from Alfaqueque* | Felipe Rivas |
| Oct | Court | *Fortunato* | Alberto |
| Nov | Strand | *Out of the Sea* | John Martin |

**1929**

| | | | |
|---|---|---|---|
| Jan | Arts | *The Seagull* | Konstantin |
| Feb | Little | *Red Dust* | Fedor |
| | Film | *The Clue of the New Pin* | |
| Mar | Prince of Wales (special perf.) | *Hunter's Moon* | Paul de Tressailles |
| Apr | Palace (special perf.) | *Shall We Show the Ladies?* | Captain Jennings |
| Apr | Garrick | *The Lady with the Lamp* | Henry Tremayne |

| June | Arts | *Red Sunday* | Bronstein (Trotsky) |
| Sept | Old Vic | *Romeo and Juliet* | Romeo |
| Oct | Old Vic | *Merchant of Venice* | Antonio |
| Oct | Old Vic | *The Imaginary Invalid* | Cléante |
| Nov | Old Vic | *Richard II* | Richard II |
| Dec | Old Vic | *A Midsummer Night's Dream* | Oberon |
| Dec | Prince of Wales (special perf.) | *Duaumont: or the Return of the Soldier Ulysses* | Prologue |

**1930**

| Jan | Old Vic | *Julius Caesar* | Mark Antony |
| Feb | Old Vic | *As You Like It* | Orlando |
| Feb | Old Vic | *Androcles and the Lion* | The Emperor |
| Mar | Old Vic | *Macbeth* | Macbeth |
| Apr | Old Vic | *The Man with the Flower in his Mouth* | Title Part |
| Apr | Old Vic | *Hamlet* | Hamlet |
| June | Queen's | *Hamlet* | Hamlet |
| July | Lyric, Hammersmith | *Importance of Being Earnest* | John Worthing |
| Sept | Old Vic | *Henry IV, Part I* | Hotspur |
| Oct | Old Vic | *The Tempest* | Prospero |
| Oct | Old Vic | *The Jealous Wife* | Lord Trinket |
| Nov | Old Vic | *Antony and Cleopatra* | Antony |

**1931**

| Jan | Sadler's Wells | *Twelfth Night* | Malvolio |
| Feb | Old Vic | *Arms and the Man* | Sergius |
| Mar | Old Vic | *Much Ado about Nothing* | Benedick |
| Apr | Old Vic | *King Lear* | Lear |
| May | His Majesty's | *The Good Companions* | Inigo Jollifant |
| Nov | Arts (special perf.) | *Musical Chairs* | Joseph Schindler |

**1932**

| Feb | OUDS | *Romeo and Juliet* | Director |
| Apr | Criterion | *Musical Chairs* | Joseph Schindler |
| May | Film | *Insult* | |
| June | Arts (special perf.) | *Richard of Bordeaux* | Richard (and director) |
| Sept | St Martin's | *Strange Orchestra* | Director |
| Oct | Film | *The Good Companions* | Inigo Jollifant |
| Dec | Old Vic | *Merchant of Venice* | Director |

**1933**

| | | | |
|---|---|---|---|
| Feb | New | *Richard of Bordeaux* | Richard (and director) |
| Sept | Wyndham's | *Sheppey* | Director |

**1934**

| | | | |
|---|---|---|---|
| Jan | Shaftesbury | *Spring, 1600* | Director |
| Apr | Tour | *Richard of Bordeaux* | |
| June | New | *Queen of Scots* | Director |
| July | Wyndham's | *The Maitlands* | Roger Maitland |
| Nov | New | *Hamlet* | Hamlet (and director) |

**1935**

| | | | |
|---|---|---|---|
| Apr | New | *The Old Ladies* | Director |
| Apr | Tour | *Hamlet* | |
| July | New | *Noah* | Noah |
| Oct | New | *Romeo and Juliet* | Mercutio (and director) |
| Nov | Film | *The Secret Agent* | |
| Nov | New | *Romeo and Juliet* | Romeo |

**1936**

| | | | |
|---|---|---|---|
| Feb | OUDS | *Richard II* | Director |
| Apr | Tour | *Romeo and Juliet* | |
| May | New | *The Seagull* | Trigorin |
| Sept | Alexandra, Toronto | *Hamlet* | Hamlet |
| Oct | St James's, New York | *Hamlet* | Hamlet |

**1937**

| | | | |
|---|---|---|---|
| Feb | Tour | *Hamlet* | Hamlet |
| Apr | Tour | *He was Born Gay* | Mason, Producer |
| May | Queen's | *He was Born Gay* | Mason, Producer |
| Sept | Queen's | *Richard II* | Richard II (and director) |
| Nov | Queen's | *The School for Scandal* | Joseph Surface |

**1938**

| | | | |
|---|---|---|---|
| Jan | Queen's | *Three Sisters* | Vershinin |
| Apr | Queen's | *Merchant of Venice* | Shylock (and director) |
| May | Ambassador's | *Spring Meeting* | Director |
| Aug | Tour | *Dear Octopus* | Nicholas |
| Sept | Queen's | *Dear Octopus* | Nicholas |

**1939**

| | | | |
|---|---|---|---|
| Jan | Globe | *Importance of Being Earnest* | John Worthing (and director) |
| Apr | Globe (special perf.) | *Scandal in Assyria* | Director |
| May | Globe | *Rhondda Roundabout* | Director |
| June | Lyceum | *Hamlet* | Hamlet (and director) |
| July | Elsinore | *Hamlet* | Hamlet (and director) |
| Aug | Globe | *Importance of Being Earnest* | John Worthing (and director) |
| Sept | Tour | *Importance of Being Earnest* | John Worthing (and director) |

**1940**

| | | | |
|---|---|---|---|
| Jan | Globe | *Importance of Being Earnest* | John Worthing (and director) |
| Mar | Haymarket | *The Beggar's Opera* | Director |
| Apr | Old Vic | *King Lear* | Lear |
| May | Old Vic | *The Tempest* | Prospero |
| July | ENSA and Tour | *Fumed Oak* | Henry Crow |
| | | *Hard Luck Story* | Old Actor |
| | | *Hands across the Sea* | Peter Gilpin |
| Oct | Film | *The Prime Minister* | Disraeli |

**1941**

| | | | |
|---|---|---|---|
| Jan | Globe | *Dear Brutus* | Dearth (and director) |
| May | Tour | *Dear Brutus* | Dearth (and director) |
| Nov | Apollo | *Ducks and Drakes* | Director |

**1942**

| | | | |
|---|---|---|---|
| Jan | Tour | *Macbeth* | Macbeth (and director) |
| July | Piccadilly | *Macbeth* | |
| Oct | Phoenix | *Importance of Being Earnest* | John Worthing (and director) |
| Dec | Gibraltar | ENSA Tour | |

**1943**

| | | | |
|---|---|---|---|
| Jan | Haymarket | *Doctor's Dilemma* | Louis Dubedat |
| Mar | Tour | *Love for Love* | Valentine (and director) |

| Apr | Phoenix and Haymarket | *Love for Love* | Valentine (and director) |
| Oct | Westminster | *Landslide* | Director |

**1944**

| Jan | Apollo | *Cradle Song* | Director |
| May | Lyric | *Crisis in Heaven* | Director |
| June | Phoenix | *Last of Summer* | Director |
| July | Tour | *Hamlet* | Hamlet |
| Aug | Tour | *Love for Love* | Valentine (and director) |
| Sept | Tour | *The Circle* | Arnold Champion-Cheney |
| Oct | Haymarket | Repertoire Season *(Hamlet, Love for Love, The Circle)* | |

**1945**

| Jan | Haymarket | *A Midsummer Night's Dream* | Oberon |
| Apr | Haymarket | *Duchess of Malfi* | Ferdinand |
| Aug | Haymarket | *Lady Windermere's Fan* | Director |
| Oct | ENSA Tour of Far East | *Hamlet* | Hamlet (and director) |
| | | *Blithe Spirit* | Charles |

**1946**

| Apr | Haymarket | *Importance of Being Earnest* | John Worthing (and director) |
| May | Tour | *Crime and Punishment* | Raskolnikoff |
| June | New and Globe | *Crime and Punishment* | Raskolnikoff |

**1947**

| Jan | Tour of Canada and US | *Importance of Being Earnest* | John Worthing (and director) |
| Mar | Royale Theatre, New York | *Importance of Being Earnest* | John Worthing (and director) |
| May | Tour of US | *Love for Love* | Valentine (and director) |
| Oct | National Theatre, N.Y. | *Medea* | Jason (and director) |
| Dec | National Theatre, N.Y. | *Crime and Punishment* | Raskolnikoff |

**1948**

| | | | |
|---|---|---|---|
| July | Haymarket | *The Glass Menagerie* | Director |
| Aug | Edinburgh Festival | *Medea* | Director |
| Sept | Globe | *Medea* | Director |
| Nov | Globe | *Return of the Prodigal* | Eustace |

**1949**

| | | | |
|---|---|---|---|
| Feb | Haymarket | *The Heiress* | Director |
| Mar | Tour | *The Lady's not for Burning* | Thomas Mendip (and director) |
| Apr | Stratford | *Much Ado about Nothing* | Director |
| May | Globe | *The Lady's not for Burning* | Thomas Mendip (and director) |
| Sept | Apollo | *Treasure Hunt* | Director |

**1950**

| | | | |
|---|---|---|---|
| Jan | Lyric, Hammersmith | *The Boy with a Cart Shall We Join the Ladies?* | Director |
| Mar | Stratford | *Measure for Measure* | Angelo |
| May | Stratford | *Julius Caesar* | Cassius |
| June | Stratford | *Much Ado about Nothing* | Benedick (and director) |
| July | Stratford | *King Lear* | Lear |

**1951**

| | | | |
|---|---|---|---|
| Jan | Royale, N.Y. | *The Lady's not for Burning* | Thomas Mendip (and director) |
| June | Brighton | *The Winter's Tale* | Leontes |
| Aug | Edinburgh Festival | *The Winter's Tale* | Leontes |
| Sept | Phoenix | *The Winter's Tale* | Leontes |

**1952**

| | | | |
|---|---|---|---|
| Jan | Phoenix | *Much Ado about Nothing* | Benedick (and director) |
| | Stratford | *Macbeth* | Director |
| Aug | Film | *Julius Caesar* | Cassius |
| Dec | Lyric, Hammersmith | *Richard II* | Director |

1953

| | | | |
|---|---|---|---|
| Feb | Lyric, Hammersmith | *The Way of the World* | Mirabell (and director) |
| May | Lyric, Hammersmith | *Venice Preserv'd* | Jaffier (and director) |
| July | Bulawayo | *Richard II* | Richard (and director) |
| Oct | Tour | *A Day by the Sea* | Julian Anson |
| Nov | Haymarket | *A Day by the Sea* | Julian Anson |
| Dec | Brighton | *Charley's Aunt* | Director |

1954

| | | | |
|---|---|---|---|
| Feb | New | *Charley's Aunt* | Director |
| May | Lyric, Hammersmith | *The Cherry Orchard* | Director |

1955

| | | | |
|---|---|---|---|
| Apr | Stratford | *Twelfth Night* | Director |
| June | Brighton | *King Lear* | Lear |
| June | European Tour | *King Lear* | Lear |
| July | Palace | *Much Ado about Nothing* | Benedick (and director) |
| July | Palace | *King Lear* | Lear |
| Aug | Film | *Round the World in Eighty Days* | Foster |
| Sept | European Tour | *King Lear* and *Much Ado* | |
| Dec | Film | *Richard III* | Clarence |

1956

| | | | |
|---|---|---|---|
| Apr | Haymarket | *The Chalk Garden* | Director |
| | Film | *The Barretts of Wimpole Street* | Mr Barrett |
| Sept | Tour | *Nude with Violin* | Sebastian (and director) |
| Nov | Globe | *Nude with Violin* | Sebastian (and co-director) |
| | Film | *St Joan* | Warwick |

1957

| | | | |
|---|---|---|---|
| June | Covent Garden | *The Trojans* | Director |
| Aug | Stratford | *The Tempest* | Prospero |
| Sept | Edinburgh Festival | *The Ages of Man* | |
| Sept | Tour | *The Ages of Man* | |
| Dec | Drury Lane | *The Tempest* | Prospero |

**1958**

| | | | |
|---|---|---|---|
| Jan | Brighton | *The Potting Shed* | James Callifer |
| Feb | Globe | *The Potting Shed* | James Callifer |
| Apr | Globe | *Variation on a Theme* | Director |
| May | Old Vic | *Henry VIII* | Wolsey |
| June | Cambridge | *Five Finger Exercise* | Director |
| Sept | Tour of Canada and US | *The Ages of Man* | |
| Dec | 46th Street Theatre, N.Y. | *The Ages of Man* | |

**1959**

| | | | |
|---|---|---|---|
| Mar | TV | *A Day by the Sea* | Julian Anson |
| Apr | CBS TV | *The Browning Version* | Andrew Crocker Harris |
| May | Tour | *The Complaisant Lover* | Director |
| June | Globe | *The Complaisant Lover* | |
| July | Queen's | *The Ages of Man* | |
| Sept | US Tour | *Much Ado about Nothing* | Director |
| Dec | Music Box, New York | *Five Finger Exercise* | Director |

**1960**

| | | | |
|---|---|---|---|
| Sept | Phoenix | *The Last Joke* | Prince Ferdinand Cavanati |

**1961**

| | | | |
|---|---|---|---|
| Feb | Covent Garden | *A Midsummer Night's Dream* | Director |
| Mar | ANTA Theatre, New York | *Big Fish, Little Fish* | Director |
| June | Globe | *Dazzling Prospect* | Director |
| Oct | Stratford | *Othello* | Othello |
| Dec | Aldwych | *The Cherry Orchard* | Gaev |

**1962**

| | | | |
|---|---|---|---|
| Apr | Haymarket | *The School for Scandal* | Director |
| Oct | Haymarket | *The School for Scandal* | Joseph Surface (and director) |
| Dec | Majestic, New York | *The School for Scandal* | Joseph Surface (and director) |

**1963**

| | | | |
|---|---|---|---|
| Jan | Majestic, New York | *The Ages of Man* | |
| June | Tour | *The Ides of March* | Caesar (and co-director) |
| Aug | Haymarket | *The Ides of March* | Caesar (and co-director) |
| Aug | TV | *The Rehearsal* | The Count |
| Sept | Film | *Becket* | Louis VII |

**1964**

| | | | |
|---|---|---|---|
| Apr | Lunt-Fontanne, New York | *Hamlet* | Director |
| May | World Tour | *The Ages of Man* | |
| Aug | Film | *The Loved One* | Sir Francis Hinsley |
| Oct | Film | *Chimes at Midnight* | Henry IV |
| Dec | Billy Rose, New York | *Tiny Alice* | Julian |

**1965**

| | | | |
|---|---|---|---|
| Aug | Tour | *Ivanov* | Ivanov (and director) |
| Sept | Phoenix | *Ivanov* | Ivanov (and director) |

**1966**

| | | | |
|---|---|---|---|
| Mar | US Tour | *Ivanov* | Ivanov (and director) |
| May | Shubert Theatre, N.Y. | *Ivanov* | Ivanov (and director) |
| July | US TV | *The Love Song of Barney Kempinski* | |
| Aug | BBC TV | *Alice in Wonderland* | Mock Turtle |
| Aug | BBC TV | *The Mayfly and the Frog* | Gabriel Kantara |

**1967**

| | | | |
|---|---|---|---|
| Jan | US Tour | *The Ages of Man* | |
| Feb | Film | *Assignment to Kill* | |
| Mar | BBC TV | *From Chekhov with Love* | Chekhov |
| Apr | Film | *Mr Sebastian* | Head of British Intelligence |
| Apr | Film | *The Charge of the Light Brigade* | Lord Raglan |
| Oct | Tour | *Half Way Up The Tree* | Director |

| Nov | Queen's | *Half Way Up The Tree* | Director |
| Nov | Old Vic (NT) | *Tartuffe* | Orgon |

**1968**

| Jan | Film | *The Shoes of the Fisherman* | The Pope |
| Feb | BBC TV | *St Joan* | Inquisitor |
| Mar | Old Vic (NT) | *Oedipus* | Oedipus |
| Apr | Film | *Oh! What a Lovely War* | Count Berchtold |
| Aug | Coliseum | *Don Giovanni* | Director |
| Oct | Apollo | *40 Years On* | Headmaster |

**1969**

| Apr | BBC TV | *In Good King Charles's Golden Days* | King Charles |
| Apr | BBC TV | *Conversation at Night* | The Writer |
| June | Film | *Julius Caesar* | Caesar |
| Oct | Film | *Eagle in a Cage* | Lord Sissal |

**1970**

| Jan | Lyric | *The Battle of Shrivings* | Sir Gideon Petrie |
| Apr | BBC TV | *Hassan* | The Caliph |
| May | ATV | *Hamlet* | Ghost |
| June | Royal Court | *Home* | Harry |
| Nov | Morosco, New York | *Home* | Harry |

**1971**

| July | Chichester | *Caesar and Cleopatra* | Caesar |

**1972**

| Mar | Royal Court | *Veterans* | Sir Geoffrey Kendle |
| Mar | Film | *Lost Horizon* | Chang |
| Aug | Queen's | *Private Lives* | Director |

**1973**

| July | Albery | *The Constant Wife* | Director |
| Sept | Film | *Eleven Harrowhouse* | Meecham |
| Oct | ATV | *Edward VII* | Disraeli |

1974
| | | | |
|---|---|---|---|
| Jan | Film | *Gold* | Farrell |
| Mar | Old Vic (NT) | *The Tempest* | Prospero |
| Apr | Film | *Murder on the Orient Express* | Beddoes |
| July | Film | *The Life of Galileo* | Cardinal |
| Aug | Royal Court | *Bingo* | Shakespeare |
| Sept | US | *Private Lives* | Director |
| Nov | Royal, York | *Paradise Lost* | Milton |
| Dec | US | *The Constant Wife* | Director |

1975
| | | | |
|---|---|---|---|
| June | Albery | *The Gay Lord Quex* | Director |
| July | Old Vic (NT) | *No Man's Land* | Spooner |
| Oct | Film | *Aces High* | Headmaster |

1976
| | | | |
|---|---|---|---|
| Jan | Film | *Caesar and Cleopatra* | Caesar |
| Apr | National Theatre (Lyttelton) | *No Man's Land* | Spooner |
| Apr | Film | *Joseph Andrews* | Doctor |
| May | Film | *Providence* | Clive |
| July | Film | *A Portrait of the Artist as a Young Man* | Preacher |
| Aug | Film | *Caligua* | Nerva |
| Nov | Longacre, New York | *No Man's Land* | Spooner |

1977
| | | | |
|---|---|---|---|
| Mar | National Theatre (Olivier) | *Julius Caesar* | Caesar |
| Apr | National Theatre (Olivier) | *Volpone* | Sir Politic Would-Be |
| Nov | Granada TV | *No Man's Land* | Spooner |
| Nov | National Theatre (Cottesloe) | *Half-Life* | Sir Noel Cunliffe |
| Dec | BBC Radio | *Romeo and Juliet* | Chorus |

1978
| | | | |
|---|---|---|---|
| Jan | BBC TV | *Richard II* | John of Gaunt |
| Feb | BBC TV | *The Cherry Orchard* | Gaev |
| Mar | Duke of York's | *Half-Life* | Sir Noel Cunliffe |

| June | Film | *Les Misérables* | Valjean's father |
| Sept | TV | *The Dame of Sark* | Butler |
| Sept | Records | *The Ages of Man* | |

**1979**

| May | Film | *The Conductor* | Title role |
| May | Film | *Omar Mukhtar* | Sheikh |
| June | Film | *The Human Factor* | Brigadier Tomlinson |
| Sept | Film | *The Elephant Man* | Carr Gomm |
| Oct | Anglia TV | *The Parson's Pleasure* | Clergyman |
| Dec | Film | *Sphinx* | Abdu |

**1980**

| Feb | Granada TV | *Brideshead Revisited* | Edward Ryder |
| | Film | *The Formula* | Dr Esau |
| Apr | Film | *Chariots of Fire* | Master of Trinity |
| May | Film | *Priest of Love* | Herbert G. Muskett |
| June | Film | *Arthur* | Hobson |
| Sept | LWTV | *Seven Dials Mystery* | Marquis of Caterham |

**1981**

| Jan | Film | *Wagner* | Counsellor to King Ludwig |
| Apr | Film | *Marco Polo* | Doge |
| July | BBC TV | *The Critic* | Lord Burleigh |
| Oct | Film | *Hunchback of Notre Dame* | Torturer |
| Nov | Film | *Inside the Third Reich* | Speer's Father |

**1982**

| Mar | Film | *Buddenbrooks* | Narrator |
| July | Film | *The Wicked Lady* | Hogarth |
| July | Film | *The Vatican Pimpernel* | Pope Pacelli |
| Aug | Film | *Invitation to a Wedding* | Texan Evangelist |
| Nov | Film | *Scandalous* | Uncle Willie |

**1983**

| Apr | HTV | *The Master of Ballantrae* | Lord Dumsdeer |
| Sept | Film | *The Shooting Party* | Cardew |

# INDEX

# INDEX

173